The Limits of Pragmatism

The Limits of Pragmatism

Carlos Gonzales, Queen's U. Kingston

C. G. Prado

 Humanities Press International, Inc.
Atlantic Highlands, NJ

First published 1987 in the United States of America by
HUMANITIES PRESS INTERNATIONAL, INC., Atlantic
Highlands, NJ 07716

Library of Congress Cataloging-in-Publication Data

Prado, C. G.
   The limits of pragmatism.

   Bibliography: p.
   Includes index.
   1. Pragmatism.   2. Knowledge, Theory of.
3. Objectivity.   I. Title.
B832.P75 1987   121   86–10612
ISBN 0–391–03455–3
ISBN 0–391–03456–1 (pbk.)

Printed in the United States of America

Contents

Preface

The preface of a philosophy book usually contains little more than acknowledgment of the author's intellectual debts and some hint of the personal side of the book's production. This brief preface has both, but, perhaps more than usual, it is important to what follows. I can make a point here that does not belong in the body of the text, where it must be made either tersely or at great length.

It is evident from my last two books that Richard Rorty's work has influenced my own very much in the past six years.[1] But while the earlier books were attempts to apply some of Rorty's views—specifically to questions about the nature of fiction and perspective change in aging—this one is largely critical of them. This reflects the greater influence on me of one of my teachers: Wallace Matson.

While I owe my first excitement with philosophy to David Everall, it was Matson who most shaped my thinking and teaching. And clearly I am still in his debt, for it was Matson who best articulated the idea that has been growing in my mind for the past couple of years and that prompted this book.[2] To phrase it as a question: Why should we think that an epistemology, an account of knowledge, must be universally applicable? Why should we think that an account of knowledge in science, for example, must serve us as well—must be the *same* account—as one in history or ethics?

The foregoing is not only the historicist lesson of our time. Part of my point is that some human knowledge may be judged to escape time and history in certain ways, once we understand how accounts of knowledge are limited by the nature of their subject matter. Rorty and other historicists think epistemology is either possible or impossible, and consider it impossible because it requires an unachievable objectivity. But epistemology may be partly attainable; objectivity may be achievable in limited ways, and therefore significantly ahistorical, though subject-specific, accounts of knowledge may be possible.

What has prevented us from seeing the possibility of limited epistemologies is that our present historicism is a universalistic one, just as the ahistoricism it displaced was universalistic. For Plato and Kant epistemology could not be limited in scope, because any account that was so limited had to be an empirical one, and hence by conception *other* than epistemological. For Rorty and most contemporaries, historicism precludes anything that is *not* empirical, and hence precludes epistemology as traditionally conceived. But there seems to be a third possibility, namely, that some of our judgments about knowledge, while remaining empirical, achieve a degree of objectivity that makes their correctness and applicability coextensive with the whole of human cognitive history. This is to say that such judgments unite human cognitive history into a single enterprise and correctly describe aspects of that enterprise irrespective of particular historical contexts. This is precisely the sense in which John Dewey and Charles Saunders Peirce thought—consistently with their pragmatism—that "inquiry" was a single progressive enterprise.

Rorty thinks that philosophy is arrogant and unviable when conceived of as the adjudicator of reason, and that epistemology is precluded by our inability to step out of language and belief. And though he is somehow very right, he is also importantly wrong—which is what this book is about. Contemporary historicism is also very right, but importantly wrong because it is haunted by the spectre of nihilistic relativism. It looks, then, as if there is not only room but also need for compromise.

To arrive at a compromise, one must begin by scrutinizing the deep assumption that philosophical accounts must be nonempirical, exhaustive, universal, and unitary. Rorty has in effect done that. But in doing so he has juxtaposed to traditional epistemology a historicist pragmatism that is as monolithic as that epistemology. In spite of his conversational liberality, he has excluded one voice: that of ahistoricism or objectivism. The main point of what follows is that pragmatism is bounded by an undeniable retrospective objectivity in some areas of knowledge. The goal is to see how pragmatism is limited—and in fact *completed*—by an emergent, restricted objectivism. In spite of its critical construal of pragmatism, I think the project is very much in the spirit of Dewey's pragmatic vision.

Notes

1. See my *Making Believe: Philosophical Reflections on Fiction*, Greenwood Press, 1984, and my *Rethinking How We Age: A New View of the Aging Mind*, Greenwood Press, 1986.

2. In a letter dated 19 February 1986, Wallace Matson perceptively notes that my exposition of Rorty shares Rorty's assumption that any epistemology, whether realist, idealist or—*pace* Rorty—pragmatic, must be universal in nature. Matson is in the process of writing a major book in which he will develop his view. His "The Pious Gene," read to the American Philosophical Association's Pacific Division meeting, January 1985, indicates the direction of his thought.

I should add that Matson's provocative ideas were complemented in a minor, but helpful, way by an M. A. thesis I am presently supervising, in which Tom Carpenter is trying to block out the way ethical theories, which are also traditionally presumed as necessarily universal in scope, fail to do justice to the complexity of the grounds of human decision.

Chapter 1

Introduction

Pragmatism survived as a philosophical position from the time of John Dewey to the late 1970s, but it did not flourish. During that period pragmatism was seldom espoused, or attributed positively, as a primary philosophical position, as it had been in the case of Dewey. Instead it was acknowledged, or attributed more critically, as an unwillingness to pursue questions and issues beyond conventional justificatory practices. Professional philosophers saw relativistic, idealistic, and nihilistic implications in pragmatism's rejection of truth as correspondence to reality. Even philosophers properly termed pragmatists, like W. V. O. Quine, were described negatively, usually to exclude one or another "foundationalist" view that human knowledge is grounded on discernible basic truths. Thus pragmatism was mainly thought of as emerging from, or being implied by, someone's work, rather than as a prior framework for that work.

In the last dozen or so years, pragmatism has been construed more often as a holistic philosophical position. This change is due largely to an increasingly historicist mood in philosophy—a mood prompted perhaps as much by the social science and literary criticism of the last several decades as by philosophical developments. But whatever the causes, there is now a rather diffuse and often unexamined pragmatism imbuing much of contemporary philosophy, especially the "applied" philosophy that has recently characterized ethics, social and political thought, and newer approaches such as feminism and the concern with nuclear issues. Truth is now conceived more historically, and as a consequence, pragmatism is more generally acknowledged as a position, rather than as a consequence of particular arguments and theses or as a methodological limit.

1

The present historicist and pragmatic intellectual mood has been articulated and fomented by a number of writers, but perhaps by none so effectively—albeit provocatively and controversially—as Richard Rorty. Rorty not only champions pragmatism in the philosophical sphere; he attempts a pragmatic erosion of the boundaries between philosophy and other areas of intellectual activity, such as literary criticism. Rorty argues that proper understanding of pragmatism's critique of traditional philosophy precludes granting philosophy a proprietary subject matter and methodology, and so explodes the myth that philosophy is the adjudicator of reason and reasoned discourse or inquiry. In this way Rorty takes himself out of the more narrowly conceived philosophical forum. He does not expound *philosophical* theses as alternatives within the sphere of traditional philosophic debate. Rather, he tries to show that philosophizing is not a special activity; that it is, in Michael Oakeshott's phrase, one more voice "in the conversation of Mankind" and hence without the privileged status to set and administer standards of rationality.

In articulating his pragmatism, Rorty captures more than the new pragmatic spirit. He also addresses a concomitant impatience with traditional correspondist and foundationalist thinking and methodology. That impatience may be integral to a philosophically viable pragmatism, or it may be only part of the relativism we have seen growing in our time. Rorty and others, like Richard Bernstein, distinguish between pragmatism and a nihilistic or simplistic relativism, which considers all beliefs equal in merit because none can be validated beyond their particular contexts. They believe that the conflation of pragmatism with such relativism is possible only if one adheres to putatively defunct correspondist and foundationalist presuppositions.

But against Rorty's view, many think that the trend toward pragmatism *is* a trend toward relativism, and better understood as an unfortunate sociological phenomenon than as intellectual progress. This controversy highlights the fact that, like any significant intellectual development, the new pragmatism—and it is in some ways new—needs to be assessed. Its growing influence, and especially its ready acceptance by many who fail to recognize it as a philosophical position, calls for critical appraisal. However, assessment poses two serious difficulties. First, it must proceed on the basis of criteria that are themselves challenged by pragmatism; second, because of its essentially critical nature, pragmatism is not readily definable.

Dealing with these difficulties requires both constant reflection on the grounds for criticizing pragmatic claims and sharp focusing on a manageable paradigmatic position. With respect to the latter, I think there is no better way to assess something as diffuse as the new pragmatism than to examine the work of one of its most effective spokespersons. But Rorty's profligacy makes even so focused an assessment an overly ambitious project. My intent in this book, therefore, is a more modest one, namely, to consider the new pragmatism, as present in Rorty's views, in one particular but elemental dimension: that of truth. In proceeding as I do I must therefore defer the study of important aspects of Rorty's work. Most notably, my focus precludes treating adequately both Rorty's relation to the Continental thinkers he admires and to some extent emulates, and his appropriation of the ideas of Dewey and William James. I touch on these matters, but cannot hope to treat them in any serious way in the present volume.

A CASE IN POINT

The most general charges against Rorty—as perhaps the most notable contemporary pragmatist, and therefore an important pragmatic critic of the mainstream philosophical tradition—are that the epistemological foundationalism he so strenuously opposes was moribund years ago, and that, in turning away from foundationalism and correspondism, Rorty wrongly insists on turning away from philosophy itself.

Even Rorty's most enthusiastic supporters wonder how to continue as philosophers if they accept Rorty's views. They ask why acknowledgment of the unworkability of Cartesian foundationalism should leave us with only so many discourses or conversations and force us to deny philosophy's disciplinary uniqueness. Nor is it only philosophy that is jeopardized. In Rorty's view, the general pragmatic denial of privileged status to any aspect of our intellectual activities affects science, too. The conception of scientific discourse, like philosophy, as just another voice in the conversation of mankind is a particularly difficult implication of Rorty's critique. The general feeling is that abandonment of Cartesian foundationalism should not reduce science to a merely narrational activity, and that rejection of correspondism and foundationalism should not preclude either a hierarchical structuring of our discourses or the hope for real progress in inquiry.

Rorty's critics feel he has overreacted against a particular and already problematic epistemological tradition by trying to end philosophy. Rorty, in abandoning correspondism (commitment to the correspondence theory of truth) and foundationalism (the epistemological view that knowledge is demonstrably grounded in pure reason or incorrigible experience), and in trying to show that we have entered a pragmatic *post*philosophical age, is criticized for relativizing and trivializing philosophical inquiry and discourse.

Rorty's insistence on the demise of traditional philosophy is perhaps not adequately understood, but there is reason for the charge of relativization and/or trivialization. For one thing, if Rorty is right, then the sort of theorizing about truth that has been conducted since Plato has been a waste of time, except insofar as it has, as a complex intellectual enterprise, enriched Western culture. However, it is too easy to read "enrichment" here as merely the provision of intellectual entertainment, since Rorty's views deny that the theorizing in question could be successful in its own terms. The Olympian perspective Rorty asks us to adopt requires us to see the history of philosophy as Friedrich Nietzsche saw it: as a chronicle of misconception rather than a progressive intellectual enterprise. Nonetheless, failure to appreciate Rorty's view of pragmatism as postphilosophical (and hence no longer *within* philosophy), masks the depth of Rorty's critique. As a result that critique is too readily accused of relativizing and even trivializing what it critiques.

Rorty's endorsement and elaboration of pragmatism is construed by many as a philosophical position, and as an acceptance of aspects of traditional pragmatism which they consider discredited. For instance, as I shall illustrate below, some criticize Rorty for accepting, implicitly or explicitly, what they see as an idealism inherent in pragmatism; that is, they think that the pragmatic rejection of epistemological foundationalism and correspondism means that the world must be of one's own making and that it must be exhausted by one's set of beliefs, since there is no means of "grounding" belief or showing it to be true. As a result, Rorty's work is often considered in a superficial and dismissive manner. But, as noted above, Rorty is trying to take a position outside of, and opposed to, traditional philosophy. Rorty reads Dewey as having succeeded at just that, and sees Dewey and himself as invulnerable to numerous philosophical appraisals, since he further assumes that full appreciation of the pragmatic critique renders traditional philosophical methodology and criteria problematic. With respect to the particular issue of truth, Rorty is not offering an alternative theory, the "pragmatic theory of truth." He maintains that the pragmatist wants to "change the subject" with respect to such issues as truth and abandon unproductive and unnecessary theorizing. We may indicate the radical nature of Rorty's work by anticipating a little the discussion of truth: Rorty seems to me less concerned with precluding or rejecting putatively ahistorical *answers* to questions such as those about truth, than he is with precluding the asking of ahistorical *questions* about anything at all. This position calls to mind Hans-Georg Gadamer's somewhat elusive understanding of truth as historical for, like Gadamer, Rorty, by allowing only historical answers, must repudiate attempts at ahistorical inquiry. That is why he speaks of turning away from theorizing about truth, for such theorizing has been intrinsically ahistorical since Plato. I think it is crucial to appreciate at the outset that the new pragmatism *is* largely a turning away from structured and especially grounded methodology. It is in this pivotal respect that Rorty's work serves us better as a focus for an assessment of contemporary pragmatism than more traditionally philosophical alternatives.

An expositor of Rorty's should try to articulate Rorty's position more convincingly than he does himself, but I do not consider myself an expositor, in spite of great sympathy for Rorty's views and my efforts to clarify some of them. Though I am drawn to Rorty's pragmatism, and convinced that it has been widely misinterpreted, I balk at some of its implications with respect to truth in general and the status of science in particular. I think I have understood how (a certain sort of) correspondism is unworkable, and how scientific theories are not ahistorically true descriptions. But I nevertheless want to give science a special place and hence acknowledge, indirectly, a form of correspondence. Moreover, I believe that philosophical inquiry has a special nature and is not merely so much more "conversation." I must, then, be a critic. However, in what follows I try to elucidate, and to some extent defend, Rorty's pragmatism as sympathetically and effectively as I can. Though it may be presumptuous, I see my struggle with Rorty's views as the contemporary struggle with pragmatism writ small, and so hope that some of my conclusions will have implications beyond my own thinking.

A PROJECT OUTLINE

Some time has passed since Rorty's two books—*Philosophy and the Mirror of Nature*[1] and *Consequences of Pragmatism*[2]—gave pragmatism new appeal and a higher profile as a philosophical position than perhaps at any time since Dewey. It is, however, too early for a satisfactory critical or historical assessment of Rorty's influence on philosophy and on intellectual life generally. And though at the time of this writing a number of people are working on systematic studies of Rorty, I suspect any comprehensive assessment of his work would be premature. But it is not too soon to consider Rorty's pragmatism with respect to the issue of truth. There is abundant material in his writings on this central topic—albeit mostly of a negative, even dismissive, nature. Moreover, it is in this area that he is least likely to advance novel proposals. Rorty has, to my mind, already said what he can about truth, or, more accurately, about how and why we should turn away from theorizing about truth. With respect to this issue Rorty is offering neither a new theory nor a new interpretation of an old theory. He is basically trying to *clarify*: specifically, to illuminate how Dewey and James allegedly put an end to philosophical puzzlement about truth; and how they revealed the unviability of the notion of "correspondence" and, by discrediting epistemological skepticism, rendered innocuous the alternative notion of "coherence."

I attempt in the following chapters to consider the core of Rorty's pragmatism: the rejection of correspondism, or the conception of truth as accurate ideational or linguistic representation of the world. I also consider Rorty's rejection of objectivism as foundationalist, that is, entailing a conception that knowledge is ultimately grounded in *a priori*, or incorrigible, experiences. In the process, I will include some *obiter dicta* on Rorty's Continental heroes and semiheroes, particularly Gadamer, although, as noted above, my objectives preclude more sustained treatment of those figures. I will consider more thoroughly the work of the philosopher Donald Davidson. In a way Davidson is Rorty's main competitor, not because he too expounds pragmatism but because his views on truth constitute the most philosophically viable alternative to the correspondence theory. In this chapter I begin with a sketch of the basic tenets and problems of pragmatism, less to instruct than to insure against misconception. In chapter 2 I discuss Rorty's position on truth in a preliminary and expository way, making some comparative remarks on Dewey's pragmatism. In the third and central chapter I consider Rorty's views on truth more carefully and draw out some implications of his attempts to read Davidson as a pragmatist. In chapter 4 I consider Rorty's pragmatism with special attention to the question of objectivity. The issue of objectivity is not separate from that of truth—it differs mainly in construal and emphasis—but charges against Rorty in particular, and pragmatism in general, often focus on the idea that pragmatism "levels" our discourses in abandoning objectivity. The dethronement of science from its privileged status is a case in point. I also consider briefly Bernstein's efforts to get past the objectivist/relativist dichotomy. The fifth and sixth chapters contain a broader assessment of pragmatism and some programmatic conclusions.

Rorty is a prolific writer, whose views have been promulgated in books, papers, lectures, and discussions. The views that concern me find fullest expression in his two books *Philosophy and the Mirror of Nature* and *Consequences of Pragmatism*. However, I will also draw on more recent papers, some of them still unpublished. I am not concerned with scholarly exposition of Rorty's views, nor do I expect my treatment of those views to coincide with his own interpretations. In spite of his continued productivity, there is a sense in which Rorty, the man, is now distanced from the work that earned him international prominence and such honors as the MacArthur Foundation award. It is now possible to argue about what Rorty thinks and about how we should interpret his writings. His writings have acquired an independent status, and it is no longer necessary—or perhaps even possible—to adjust our interpretation of them in response to their author's judgments. We can consider Rorty's work without having his approval of our interpretation. And that work represents, in my estimation, the most compelling elaboration of pragmatism since Dewey's.

To recapitulate, this book intends to assess contemporary pragmatism with respect to its most elemental tenet, its position on truth. To accomplish this, I will examine Rorty's views on truth and objectivity. My aim is to approach an evaluation of what Bernstein describes as the present trend toward "a more historically situated, nonalgorithmic, flexible understanding of human rationality."[3] To proceed I must first offer a brief characterization of pragmatism, if only to prevent some of the more common misconceptions about that most misunderstood and mistrusted philosophical position.

THE COMMON VIEW OF PRAGMATISM

Pragmatism is usually introduced to philosophy students as a third alternative to the correspondence and coherence theories of truth. And its introduction is often qualified by the suggestion that it is a poor third, while coherence is rated a poor second. Moreover, pragmatism and coherence are commonly described as *philosophical* alternatives to correspondence, and therefore interesting only as abstract positions, not as real options. What prompts the negative attitude toward pragmatism is a prejudice for correspondence which is not difficult to understand, because the correspondence conception of truth is fundamental to our present form of life. Alfred Tarski's semantic theory of truth, that "Snow is white" is true if and only if snow is white, will seem pleonastic to the layman, and is eminently intelligible in a way other philosophical theses are not. Everyone understands that sentences are true if they accurately capture "the facts" and take truth-as-correspondence to be unquestionable. When pragmatism is introduced in terms of the pragmatic theory of truth—usually as the thesis that truth is "what works" (James)—people take it as a kind of philosophical exaggeration. They fail to fully appreciate the pragmatic position as an alternative to correspondism. This is most evident in the objection to the pragmatic theory which first-year students so readily produce: namely, that what works, and is described as pragmatically "true," works only because it is really true according to correspondence. The result is that attention focuses on pragmatism as a dubious theory of truth, and there is failure to take seriously the pragmatist challenge to the correspondist philosophical tradition.

Anyone who has taught introductory philosophy knows how difficult it is to persuade students to accept the pragmatic theory as a viable account of truth in its own right because of resistance arising from "folk correspondism." But philosophical prejudice is also very real, and too many who teach introductory philosophy have little interest in bringing out the legitimacy of pragmatism. As a result, pragmatism is often disparaged by an invidious juxtaposition to the correspondence theory of truth. The few who delve more deeply into Dewey—or James or C. S. Peirce—are surprised that there is more to pragmatism than either an account of truth given in some brief textbook treatment or a vaguely defined practicality illustrated with one or another truncated selection. But for most, pragmatism remains a philosophical oddity, rather like Malebranche's interventionism or Meinong's notion of subsistence.

A philosopher who tries to explicate how pragmatism is a serious position immediately faces a problem Rorty has neatly captured:[4] the paradoxical need to use nonpragmatic language to lend weight to the characterization, while not allowing the language of the philosophical establishment to distort the pragmatic content of what is being said. This problem is due to the inherent correspondist nature of mainstream philosophical discourse since Plato and Aristotle.

Putting things in the most general way, pragmatism is a rejection of the entire "foundationalist" philosophical tradition that aspires to discern an ahistorical truth on which to ground human knowledge. Pragmatism as a philosophical position focuses on the correspondence theory, the basic tenet of which is that all true sentences share a unique feature or property, namely, correspondence to "the facts." This is not simply the mundane notion that we can say how things are. It is an essentially *theoretical* notion that there is a special relatedness between true sentences and how things are, a relatedness named, and to some extent described by, "correspondence." But the correspondence theory and pragmatism are not two contenders in the same debate on truth. Pragmatism is a philosophical stance at odds with correspondism, not as a competing theory of truth but as a rejection of the need for such a theory. The pragmatist sees nothing to be gained by pursuing theories of truth, in particular, elaborations of the relation of correspondence, for we will never be able to confirm a relation of correspondence—or its lack. Therefore the pragmatist is not a competing theorist; she wants to abandon theorizing about truth altogether. This is precisely what discussions of pragmatism overlook when conducted within the confines of talk about truth. But pragmatism is neither an underdog in the truth-theory race nor a vaguely conceived tough-mindedness best suited to practical concerns.

CHARACTERIZING PRAGMATISM

The most succinct general account of pragmatism I have found is Phillip Wiener's.[5] Wiener attributes to pragmatism four central tenets: a pluralistic empiricism, a temporalistic view of reality, a contextualist conception of reality and values, and a secular democratic individualism. These tenets require further explanation but in what follows I offer my interpretation of each, rather than rely strictly on Wiener's own amplifications.

A pluralistic empiricism is first of all a rejection of *a priorism*, but without a corresponding doctrinaire commitment to "experience" as the sole source of knowledge. The latter qualification suggests an important distinction between pragmatism's epistemological aspect and classical empiricism. The point is that pragmatism accepts a variety of accounts of knowledge and of the criteria for knowledge. There is as much resistance to the idea that we sufficiently understand the notion of "experience" to restrict the sources of knowledge to it, as there is to the idea that ahistorical and singular knowledge is available *a priori*. The heart of the pragmatic claim is that the criteria for knowledge are inherently societal and historical, and there can be no prior determination of its sources or limits. What counts as knowledge may change, as may what counts as justification for belief. This is a point to be explored at greater length below; it suffices to note here that a central characteristic of pragmatism is the rejection of *a priorism* both as a source of knowledge and as a restriction of sources of knowledge.

The second tenet, the temporalistic view of reality and knowledge, overlaps the first. What counts as "reality" or as "knowledge" is a matter of historical context. This espousal of historicism rejects access to a determinate reality that somehow underlies, and grounds judgments about, the world, thereby rendering at least some of them ahistorical and foundational with respect to others. But note that reality is not at issue, only our access to it, and the coherence of the notion that an accessible reality, independent of our constructs, serves to ground judgments and beliefs. This point leads to the third tenet, the contextualistic conception of reality and values, whose point is precisely that "reality" is what is counted as such in a particular historical context. Again, this is not to deny reality or value in some "heavy" ontological way, as some simplistic interpretations of pragmatism would have it. It is to say that we take to be real and of value what our time and place lead us to.

Admittedly, most people will object to the foregoing remarks and will insist that, after all, the world is as it is regardless of what we think. The world was never flat, in spite of popular conviction and social criteria for truth. What needs to be emphasized here is that the dispute is not about the world but about what we say and believe about it. Moreover, these are everything to us, for when the world surprises us, as it does when we do not fall off its edge, occurrences are mediated by our beliefs and expectations. If the events are dramatic enough to initiate an epistemological crisis that necessitates a radical change in our belief structure, the new structure will consist of so many more beliefs. In a sense, the core of pragmatism is that we ought never assume that there will be no more surprises, crises, or changes in belief structure. When the earth was thought flat, and seamen found themselves far beyond where the edge should have been, beliefs and criteria for correctness had to change. But the changes came about because of what people were willing to say and believe. Had they insisted, as some still claim to do, that the world is indeed flat, they could have readjusted their beliefs to allow for odd events. As Quine might point out, it all depends on what you are willing to give up.[6] Pragmatism denies the possibility of settling such disputes once and for all by appeal to *how the world is* independently of our beliefs, for pragmatism denies a Truth that transcends belief.

The fourth tenet, secular democratic individualism, is most relevant to political and social issues and might be more adequately described in terms of pluralism. Roughly, this tenet opposes the exclusion or subjugation of the individual in social and political realms on the basis of overriding principles, values, or objectives. By rejecting transcendent values or principles as grounds for institutional aims and practices, it rejects totalitarianism. This states the point somewhat differently from Wiener, whose characterization seems to me freighted with political individualism. Nonetheless, what is central is the repudiation of transcendent justification for the curtailment of individual participation in the social and political spheres.

The fourth aspect of pragmatism is most familiar to North Americans, with this distortion: when individuals or institutions are considered "pragmatic," they are thought not only to eschew claims of transcendent value or justification, but also to be prone to compromise and adjustment. This is a distortion because such flexibility is invariably associated by lay people with lack of "principle." However, rejection of divine right or the overriding authority of The State is not at all incompatible with holding principles. The point is only that no principle is absolute; unfortunately, few lay people understand that principles can operate in spite of this. Actually, once this particular lesson is learned, pragmatism becomes intellectually compelling, for the main obstacles to it are the yoked ideas that truth cannot be truth unless it is ahistorical and that principle cannot be principle unless it is absolute.

What is to be noted about the foregoing tenets is that they are essentially negative. That is, they are rejections of philosophical positions and theses rather than theses or positions themselves. If this point is not appreciated, pragmatism will inevitably be misconceived as a philosophical position competing with others such as idealism. But pragmatism is a philosophical position only in a special sense: it is primarily a preclusion of certain kinds of philosophical positions, namely, those involving recourse to putative ahistorical truth, immutable epistemological foundations, knowable ultimate ontological truths, and so on. This is why the philosophical tradition had so much trouble with Dewey's later work, and why it is having so much trouble with Rorty. Philosophers within the tradition insist on reading the pragmatist's pronouncements as philosophical theses and assessing them by established philosophical standards. The pragmatist is able to circumvent such criticism by more or less ignoring it, and being content to reach those not committed to the established tradition. Rorty points out that pragmatists are not obliged to take up the vocabularies and criteria of their opponents, and that they may succeed simply in offering a productive alternative to whatever tradition they oppose.[7] However, while this approach may be satisfactory to those who are willing to ignore the philosophical tradition, it is not so to those, like myself, who value some of the tradition's aspects and aspire to break through some of its more hidebound dogmas. The result is that serious efforts must be made to articulate the pragmatic stance in a way that makes it accessible to those within the tradition it opposes.

MAJOR DIFFICULTIES

Pragmatism has been charged with nihilism and vicious relativism. Underlying both accusations is the argument that pragmatism robs us of all grounds for priorities among our beliefs and values. The charge of nihilism emphasizes that the rejection of ahistorical truth and objectivity results in the trivialization and leveling of values. The accusation of vicious relativism claims that when external, objective criteria for correctness are abandoned, the only possible result is a hopeless cognitive relativism or subjectivism. The latter argument often maintains that pragmatism collapses into idealism when truth is abandoned.. Thus, the main difficulties of pragmatism concern what we lose when we forsake ultimate truth and value; and such concerns arise from the fear that rejection of objective truth and objectivity leaves us with no way to justify our judgments that some things are better than others or that things are as we take them to be.

The charge of vicious relativism is the philosophically simpler and can be sketched briefly. It argues that the abandonment of foundationalism in epistemology—or the abandonment of epistemology itself—is identical with relativism regarding belief. By giving up truth as an absolute standard, the pragmatist loses the capacity to properly prioritize beliefs. To the critic, once truth is relativized to societal norms, or to anything else, then all beliefs must be held equal. Wallace Matson once jokingly called this "the argument from democracy."[8] The force and significance of societal consensus is overlooked here, but that is not surprising in a philosophical tradition that despises the common and insists on considering only the logical and conceptual—where the conceptual is conceived as ahistorical on the model of the logical.

The argument that pragmatism is inherently relativistic in a self-vitiating way takes various forms. As mentioned above, a common claim is that pragmatism is implicitly idealistic. Pragmatists are accused of making "how things are" contingent on belief when foundationalism and epistemological realism are rejected. A paradigmatic instance of this is

Hugo Meynell's argument that Rorty is committed to idealism because he makes truth turn on societal agreement, thereby making facticity contingent on societal agreement.[9] Meynell misinterprets Tarski's semantic theory of truth as an account of correspondence and claims that acceptance of Tarski's formulation makes clear that, given the dependence of truth on facticity, if Rorty makes truth depend on societal agreement, he must be making facticity depend on societal agreement. This point may seem devastating at first glance, and will appeal to anyone who has read Rorty unsympathetically or superficially. Since the truth of "Snow is white" depends on snow being white, if Rorty makes that truth turn on societal agreement, he must be making the whiteness of snow turn on such agreement. Meynell retains the *relata* of the correspondence relation in order to charge Rorty with reversing their order of dependency. That is, Meynell retains truth and facticity and argues that since truth depends on facticity, if Rorty or anyone else gives priority to truth in a new societal account of truth, then he must make facticity dependent on societal truth.

First of all, as noted, Meynell interprets Tarski's theory, which is about meaning and relations among sentences, as relating sentences to brute facts. Second, Meynell misconstrues Rorty on truth, for Rorty is offering neither a theory of truth nor societal agreement as an analysis of truth. Rorty wants to change the subject. Without a philosophical theory of truth as its focus, the implications of Meynell's argument are nonexistent. But more important, Meynell begs the question against Rorty, and pragmatists generally, by presupposing that true sentences and facticity are juxtaposed as in the correspondence theory of truth. Meynell assumes facticity as a *relatum* when contrasting it with Rorty's societal truth. Meynell describes Rorty, and by implication any pragmatist, as saying that things are as they are believed to be, when they are saying only that things are believed to be as they are believed to be, and that trying to say how they *are* (in the sense in question) is a pointless exercise. Reading Rorty as he does, Meynell precludes the possibility of pragmatism by conflating it with idealism, which does offer a competing theory of truth. Moreover, Meynell's argument, and others like it, presupposes that Tarski's formulation somehow transcends language to capture the relation of correspondence. Tarski offered what Donald Davidson and Rorty assume he offered: namely, a way of understanding how "a natural language [is] a learnable, recursive structure . . . ."[10] Tarski did not propose a way of articulating how language "hooks on" to the world. His formulation captures what it means to say, *within language*, that a sentence is true. The sentence "Snow is white" is juxtaposed not to the brute whiteness of snow, whatever that may be, but to what speakers of English consider to be the truth conditions for the sentence.

However arcane its epistemological versions become, the charge of vicious relativism is just the claim that, without truth or objectivity untainted by context or belief, correctness and appraisal criteria become internal to sets of beliefs or discourses; and without external assessment such sets of beliefs and discourses float free of one another. They also float free of what many accept as uncontroversial, evident truths about how the world is and about what is good.

The charge of nihilism is more complex, if only because it overflows the boundaries of epistemological and metaphysical discussion. For one thing, it is as likely to be leveled by a layperson as by a philosopher; for another, it is couched in terms of value and therefore involves notoriously complex notions. The basic idea differs little from the relativism charge recast in epistemological terms: namely, once absolute value is abandoned, and the notion of value is relativized, then there is no adequate reason to favor one value over another. For the critic, discussions of values are merely attempts to persuade, and philosophical discourse is "just talk," something we engage in because it amuses us. This point has been made repeatedly in reviews and discussions of Rorty's recent work.[11] Nor is the charge limited to the very general topic of values as such. There are ongoing discussions of a much more focused sort. For instance, in connection with the philosophy of literature, the critic of pragmatism worries that we will be unable to say with any authority that one novel is better than another. This assumes that the pragmatist must argue that even the poorest yarn might be accorded great significance by some societal group, or prove more useful in some way than a novel now deemed superior.

Most of the debates about nihilism are of a reductivist/antireductivist form, such as that between behaviorists and so-called mentalists. Against the claim that mental-term ascriptions are only complex references to behavior, the mentalist argues that behaviorism ignores what it is to be the subject of mental states, to feel anger or expectation; that no amount of talk about what one does can adequately convey what one experiences. Similarly, the critic of pragmatism argues that no amount of talk about what is valued can capture what merits being valued. Without truth and value as at least absolute limiting cases, value-talk can only be about what is valued or what might be valued, but never about what should be valued.

There is another aspect to the charge of nihilism, evident in Bernstein's review of Rorty's *Mirror*, which has more to do with the role of the philosopher than with value as such. Bernstein complains that Rorty leaves us with all the tough problems about how to live.[12] The philosopher, who like Rorty is a pragmatist, abrogates responsibility by failing to propound positive theses. And of course he cannot pronounce on value if he abdicates the position of adjudicator of reason and limner of ultimacies. The pragmatic philosopher becomes one more participant in conversation, with no more—and no less—authority than fellow participants. And that discomfits people who need or want pronouncements of an absolute sort.

SKETCHING A RESPONSE

In this section I want to outline broadly how Rorty as a representative pragmatist would respond to the charges of vicious relativism and nihilism. My intention is to defend and clarify Rorty's pragmatism.

Both accusations against pragmatism—nihilism and vicious relativism—are about foundations; both are direct reactions against pragmatism's rejection of foundationalism. "Without Truth there can be no truths; without Value there can be no values" is a doctrine that articulates a profound need for foundations. Because of that need, the history of philosophy can be described as footnotes to Plato instead of to Heraclitus.

The major difficulty in dealing with foundationalist charges is that doing so requires the defeat, or at least the suspension of very deep presuppositions. Moreover, the depth of these presuppositions makes it difficult to recognize them. Usually they are treated as "conceptual truths" admitting of no alternative. The pragmatist, then, is said to be evading the issue if she recasts a charge or question in terms more suitable to her claims and position.

There is no better instance of these presuppositions than that concerning truth. The relation of true sentences to "the facts" is presupposed at so deep a level that the pragmatist's rejection of the correspondence theory of truth is considered at best paradoxical and at worst perverse. It is thought absurd to suggest that there is no relation of "correspondence" between what we believe and say about the world and how the world exists independent of our beliefs and sayings. Philosophers invariably counter pragmatic reservations and critiques with appeals to allegedly simple and self-evident cases, such as that the sentence "The coffee cup is on the table" is undeniably true in virtue of a coffee cup's obvious position on a table. As I have said elsewhere,[13] it seems that in such cases the correspondence relation is palpable and we can all but see how the sentence we utter relates to the fact. The trouble is that we never *do* see that; we never climb out of language and belief and observe their relatedness to how things are outside language and belief. At best we produce paradigms of Tarski's semantic theory. But what Tarski's theory yields, as I noted earlier and supported with the reference to Rorty and Davidson, is only what it means to say a sentence is true.[14] Tarski did not succeed—assuming he intended to try—at escaping language in order to relate particular sentences to particular juxtapositions of the world's furniture.

Perhaps we can make a little progress here by borrowing from Ian Hacking's admirably succinct remarks on Davidson's views on truth. In this way I can also introduce these views, which will be considered more carefully in the third chapter.

Hacking describes Davidson's conception of truth as compatible with pragmatism because it is not correspondist in the traditional sense, but is at the same time adequate to the strongly held view that truth must be some sort of correspondence. Hacking tells us that

> Davidson . . . defends "what may as well be called a coherence theory of truth and knowledge which is not in competition with a correspondence theory, but depends for its defense on an argument that purports to show that coherence yields correspondence. . . . " In conjecturing a theory of truth about the speech of another person, we must . . . arrange for him a coherent bundle of beliefs and utterances, coherent by our lights, the only lights we have. *But what we call reality is not something that can be identified independently of how we identify it.* Hence that which we, by using the standard of coherence, call true, unsurprisingly, and vacuously, "corresponds" to the world. . . . Davidson's correspondence, shorn of reference, does not copy a given reality.[15]

Davidson is not happy to be called a pragmatist, and there is a clear sense in which he is not. For one thing, Davidson is offering theories in a way, and of a sort, that Rorty and Dewey would see as aspiring to ahistorical status. But Davidson does offer an insightful way of construing what is so powerful in the correspondence theory: the idea that our language relates to how things are. And he avoids the traditional mistake of thinking the relation is some sort of isomorphism mediated by reference, by a way language has of "hooking on" to the world. If we jettison the dubious idea of reference, and with it the "copy" view of correspondence, we realize we cannot deny that language, as a whole, is about the world, insofar as it is how we deal with the world. As Hacking puts it, individual sentences do not "correspond" to individual facts, rather

> the whole web of sentences has to be true to the one fact, that is, the fact of everything. . . . There is only total correspondence of all true sentences to the fact of everything; but this fact, the world, has no autonomy beyond what we say. That is one way in which "coherence yields correspondence."[16]

Correspondence is inevitably a code word for Cartesian certainty. Instead of pushing for replacement of the correspondence theory with "warranted assertibility" (Dewey) or "what works" (James), contemporary pragmatists should be content to show the emptiness of the traditional notion of correspondence and the unworkable epistemology that underlies it. Rorty admittedly had this as his objective, but his work would be better received if his provocative rejection of correspondence were more clearly an argument against the possibility of epistemic certainty.[17] That is, his treatment of capital-T Truth, the unacceptable copy theory, and lower-case-t truth, which simply reflects the criteria of a linguistic community, might be more effectively presented as a rejection of a Cartesian sort of truth-as-epistemic-certainty, and an endorsement of truth as it is used in discourse untainted by philosophical theorizing. The latter sort of truth becomes the former sort when foundationalist theorizing tries to "ground" in epistemic certainty what is ordinarily said about things being true or false. Such theorizing surreptitiously introduces capital-T Truth as that possessed when epistemic certainty is achieved. Capital-T Truth is introduced, then treated as the fundamental sort from which more mundane truths derive. This is a typical philosophical move: the introduction of something which is subsequently hailed as the essence of the ordinary.

It is because capital-T Truth is foisted on us by philosophers seeking Cartesian certainty that arguments against such Truth inevitably fail. A kind of deconstruction of the notion is needed to show how it comes to be used as it is. That is what Rorty has attempted: a many-sided discussion of Truth that intends to expose the notion as a bogus one, and to show that it is *ad hoc* in being designed to embody sought-for epistemic certainty.

Rorty's critique of correspondence is astute, but Davidson's hat trick, in which he pulls correspondence out of coherence, is arguably preferable to Rorty's many-sided attack. Davidson gives us the "correspondence" we want so much, but demonstrates that it is worth having only in a trivial way, or at least in a way that does not support foundationalist philosophizing. I think Rorty and Davidson must agree in the end, and would probably be bored by further discussion of truth. But at this point Rorty too often sounds as if he is taking something from us, while Davidson is showing us its real nature and worth.

Mention of epistemic certainty raises the possibility of misconstruing Rorty, and pragmatists generally, as epistemologizing truth. They do not argue that truth and epistemic certainty are unattainable limiting points on a continuum, and that warranted assertibility, for instance, is an attainable point on that same continuum. This misunderstanding is unfortunately supported by aspects of classical pragmatism such as Peirce's interpretation of scientific method as *inevitably* leading to consensus and progress, as if inquiry were on a fixed path to a point just short of truth. Dewey seems to have shared this view to some extent, and Rorty gave some credence to it in *Mirror*, but has since explicitly repudiated it.[18] I shall return to this point in considering both Rorty's relation to Dewey and objectivity in science.

The Rortyan pragmatist holds that notions such as warranted assertibility should *displace* that of truth. This point is missed if one reads the "warranted" in "warranted assertibility" as meaning "well grounded" or "justified" in the sense of supported by evidence. "Warranted," at least for Rorty, means "allowed" or "proper" in the sense of being an appropriate move in a language game; it is what our interlocutors will "let us get away with." This is why the charge of relativism is more worrying for Rorty than for, say, Peirce, and why Rorty puts so much stress on the Wittgensteinian language-game nature of our discourses. It is also why so many of his critics feel he ends up with *just* language games.

But to return to the matter at hand, the progress we make in considering Davidson, even in this preliminary way, is that we realize there can be challenges to capital-T Truth which are neither coherence views in the traditional sense, nor pragmatic alternatives of the most familiar sort. We learn from Davidson that there is a sense in which truth is correspondence and true sentences relate to the world, but not because true sentences are faithful portraits of facts or how the world is arranged.

The most suspect notion in the unworkable "copy" theory is what Quine was so concerned to defeat, namely, the idea of a kind of unfailing referentiality, in which at least some words or sentences link up in a very tight way to bits of the world. Muddles about truths arise in this notion that, aside from how we use words and sentences, there is some way they "hook up" to what they are used to describe. Once that notion is accepted, once reference is taken as our bridge to the world, truth-as-correspondence in some sort of "copy" sense is unavoidable. Once words and sentences are thought to have "hard" reference, they can be juxtaposed to the world in only one of two ways: either in a way that replicates the arrangement of their referents, or in a way that fails to. We can go back to Plato's *Theaetetus* and *Sophist* to see a paradigmatic statement of this inevitable view.[19] Plato speaks of phrases such as "Theaetetus sits" and "Theaetetus flies" as true or false in virtue of replicating actual or nonexistent "combinations" of Forms, that is, of "hard" referents. And it is difficult to see how else words and sentences might work once we accept that they can only work at all because of reference.

The essence of the foregoing remarks is that the charge of vicious relativism leveled against pragmatism depends on a misinterpretation of the pragmatist's stand on truth. If the basic structure of the correspondence theory of truth is retained, which is to say that if pragmatism is either dismissed or misconstrued, then it is easy to argue that the pragmatic critique of capital-T Truth is vulnerable to the charge in question. The only thing a misconstrued pragmatism is allowed to do with truth is make it relative to belief or convention. But the point of the pragmatic critique is not to offer a new analysis of truth. The point is to make us scrutinize the correspondence view of truth and see that it cannot be successfully defended, for we can never get out of language or our beliefs. The world—brute reality—is simply not accessible to us as a standard against which we can check our descriptive sentences. When this is understood, a more sophisticated problem arises, namely, that the notion of reference is as illusory as that of correspondence, for we can never establish that a word or sentence "hooks up" to just *this* or just *that*, whether these be things or events. So the whole picture of language as capable of symbolic replication dissolves into paradox. What is left is language as a way of coping. Both Davidson and Rorty agree on that much. What divides them, as we shall see in chapter 3, is whether there is anything *more* to be said.

The only way we have of "catching up" bits of the world and what goes on in it is in language—symbolically. Experience is fleeting, and it is remembered symbolically, not relived. If it were, it could not be the object of reflection that it so clearly is. But when we "catch up" bits of the world or what goes on in it, we do not do so by acquiring linguistic *simulacra*, which can be checked for accuracy against their originals. The pragmatist wants us to understand that we cannot talk about "correspondence" because we are restricted to one end of the relation. The depth of Davidson's view is that he understands how, in spite of being limited to one end of the relation, we can say that the whole of language does "correspond" to the way things are.

The main response to the charge of relativism states that pragmatism is viciously relativistic only if the very conception of truth which it rejects is retained as the basis for the charge. But I have carefully spoken of "vicious" relativism, because I think that pragmatism is properly perspectivistic, and perspectivism is a sort of relativism—at least in the view of the philosophical tradition. But while relativism can be self-vitiating and stultifying, it can also be, as perspectivism, a quiet acknowledgment that we must forget about what we have never had and can never attain: epistemic bedrock on which to ground the single *true* perspective.

Defending pragmatism from the charge of vicious relativism is difficult and complex, but dealing with the accusation of nihilism is even more so, for it involves dimensions well beyond the discursive. There is a sense in which the charge cannot be met without a perspective on reality that requires neither transcendencies nor ultimacies to guarantee that what we prize most is worthy of being prized. I see this as an essentially theological issue, in that the challenge is prompted by a metaphysical felt-need rather than by rational doubt. The pragmatist says that the values we have are the values we have; they are not problematic because they are our values, rather than values external to us. But some see the grounding of value in what we want as a complete and hopeless relativization and trivialization of value, and hence as a replacement of value with "mere" preference.

One need not invoke Ludwig Feuerbach to say that what we deem to be of transcendent value is only what we project out into the world, and then take back into ourselves as objective worth. We distrust our own constancy. And we feel that if what is of value is independent of us, then it can be relied on to remain of value. The alleged alternative is that if value is only valuing, then it must be "arbitrary" and subject to whim. So we invent God, or The Good, or Pure Reason. The pragmatist wants to break this vicious circle, to recognize value in its own right, not because it comes from outside. But the nonpragmatist, driven by the need to objectify value, sees any qualification of ultimacy as leading only to caprice. The consequence is that pragmatic arguments are not construed as critiques of our prevailing conception of value, but rather as directed against *value*.

The basic argument against the charge of nihilism is that value is not lessened by being seen as a product of human aspirations, practices, and objectives. But this is not considered a proper response, for the presupposition is that any attempt to make value less than wholly objective must be a qualification of value itself. The reason is that the prevailing conception begins with the idea that value is objective, and therefore disallows that value might be only a conception.

The foregoing remarks are intended as little more than scene-setting, a sketch of issues central to pragmatism and a programmatic indication of the pragmatist's responses. In the next chapter I begin my consideration of the key issue of truth with a characterization of Rorty's position.

Notes

1. Richard Rorty, *Philosophy and the Mirror of Nature* (Princeton: Princeton University Press, 1979).
2. Richard Rorty, *Consequences of Pragmatism* (Minneapolis: University of Minnesota Press, 1982).
3. Richard Bernstein, *Beyond Objectivism and Relativism: Science, Hermeneutics and Praxis* (Philadelphia: University of Pennsylvania Press, 1983), xi.
4. Rorty, *Consequences*, xiv.
5. Phillip Wiener, "Pragmatism," in *Dictionary of the History of Ideas*, ed. Wiener (New York: Charles Scribner's Sons, 1973), 551–70.
6. Willard van Orman Quine, "Two Dogmas of Empiricism," reprinted in Quine, *From a Logical Point of View*, 2d ed. (Cambridge: Harvard University Press, 1961).
7. Rorty, *Consequences*, 156.
8. In a lecture, University of California, Berkeley, 1961.
9. Hugo Meynell, "Reversing Rorty," read at Queen's University, Kingston, Ontario, 6 December 1984. Forthcoming in *Method*. See also Hugo Meynell, "Scepticism Reconsidered," *Philosophy* 59 (1984): 431–42.
10. Rorty, *Consequences*, xxvi.
11. See, e.g., Richard Bernstein, "Philosophy in the Conversation of Mankind," *The Review of Metaphysics* 33 (1980): 745–76. See also John Caputo, "The Thought of Being and the Conversation of Mankind: the Case of Heidegger and Rorty," *The Review of Metaphysics* 36 (1983): 661–85; Isaac Levi, "Escape from Boredom: Edification According to Rorty," *Canadian Journal of Philosophy* 11 (1981): 589–601.
12. Bernstein, "Conversation," 745–76.
13. C. G. Prado, "Rorty's Pragmatism," *Dialogue* 22 (1983): 441–50.
14. See note 10, above.
15. Ian Hacking, "On the Frontier," *The New York Review*, 20 December 1984.
16. Ibid.

17. I owe the point to E. J. Bond.
18. Richard Rorty, "Pragmatism, Davidson and Truth," forthcoming in a *Festschrift* for Davidson edited by Ernest LePore, to be published by University of Minnesota Press, 10 n. 8. Note that page references are to a photocopied draft. Used with permission.
19. See, for example, Plato, *Sophist*, 259D–261C, and especially 262E–263B, in Francis Cornford, *Plato's Theory of Knowledge* (Indianapolis: Bobbs-Merrill, 1957).

Chapter 2

The Denial of Truth

PRELIMINARY REMARKS

The critical aspects of Rorty's pragmatism center on the rejection of foundationalism, and that in turn centers on the rejection of the correspondence theory of truth. Correspondism is the foundation of foundationalism, and an attack on correspondism must be an attack on all forms of philosophical foundationalism. While Rorty's discussions are not limited to the issue of truth—his positive efforts focus on hermeneutics and edification—the heart of his critique of traditional philosophy is rejection of the correspondence theory of truth.

Rorty's rejection of correspondism may be considered more eclectic and summational than novel. His polemic against it may be characterized as a synthesis of reservations and criticisms that have been present in philosophy for some time. Or it may be construed more narrowly as a refurbished version of some particular anticorrespondist view, such as the truth-is-not-a-property thesis expounded some two decades ago by philosophers like Peter Strawson. Were these appraisals correct, there would be little reason to consider Rorty's views on truth in detail. But I do not think them correct. As will become clear, Rorty's rejection of correspondism merits attention for a number of reasons. First, as I suggest below, his conception of correspondence is special; second, the implications for science of his views on truth are extremely serious; and third, unlike views such as those of Strawson, the consequences of Rorty's views on truth for philosophical methodology and argument are substantial.

If philosophers abandon correspondism for Rorty's reasons, they must acknowledge that philosophical theorizing about truth, which is fundamental to traditional philosophizing, is futile and misconceived. As a consequence, they are left without a discipline or the possibility of an objective methodology. The force of Rorty's pragmatism is that philosophizing as traditionally conducted becomes little more than an arcane game, for it cannot *advance* our understanding. Instead it is at best part of the determination of what we will count as understanding. To abandon the possibility of theorizing about truth is to concede that philosophical theorizing in general is not and cannot be progressive, except in the sense that it contributes to the constitution of our epochal justificatory procedures and the conception of our intellectual projects.

In my view, Rorty's pragmatic rejection of correspondism and the attendant refusal to allow privileged status to any discourse are more important than his much-discussed endorsement of hermeneutics. This is in part because the endorsement of hermeneutics is a *consequence* of the rejection of correspondism, for that endorsement is all that is left to espouse of intellectual activity of the sort usually described as philosophical. Many see Rorty's turn away from "analytic" philosophy toward Continental thought as the embrace of a competing alternative. Rather, the rejection of correspondence leaves only hermeneutics, not as an alternative but as the alleged initial stage of intellectual activity freed from the obsessions of Plato, Descartes, and Kant. Rorty often sounds tolerant of the continuation of traditional philosophy, and even allows that it might be significantly refurbished. But that is something of a facade, for to continue doing traditional philosophy is really to miss the point of pragmatic criticism. Appreciation of pragmatism is in the full sense a loss of innocence; one cannot go back. And appreciation of pragmatism begins with full realization of the hopelessness of correspondism. Loss of faith in capital-T Truth is like loss of faith in God, and the rejection of correspondism is a perverse sort of proselytizing, for it attempts to remove the single most important support for faith in philosophy as a uniquely criteriological enterprise, if not as the adjudicator of reason.

My aim in this chapter is largely expository, but I will limit discussion of Rorty's brand of pragmatism to the central rejection of correspondence. One can construe Rorty's efforts regarding thinkers like Gadamer and Jacques Derrida, either as a sophisticated discipleship or as what I think they are, namely, Rorty's attempts to engage in and illustrate postphilosophical intellectual activity, where "philosophical" refers mainly to Platonic and Kantian methodology and objectives. However intriguing we may find Rorty's interest in and support of much that is now being popularly received from the Continent, I think the more important issue, and Rorty's more lasting critical contribution, concerns what philosophers decide to say about truth. The impatience with ahistorical truth that I spoke of earlier should not blind us to the fact that what is most crucially at stake at the present time is our conception of truth—and this is because we can no longer unreservedly accept the sense of truth Plato, Descartes, and Kant shared. Concern with truth is exemplified by Davidson's efforts to say how truth is not piecemeal replication of an immutable reality. But the significance of Davidson's ongoing work, as of the implicit commitments and difficulties faced by historicists like Gadamer, is that we do not yet have in place an alternative to correspondence. Davidson is trying to understand what we should say about truth because he understands that the facile relativism so many espouse will not do. And in pursuing a workable account of truth, Davidson is philosophizing. Rorty wants us to give up that project as simply unproductive. His rejection of correspondence is the heart of his repudiation of traditional philosophy, for without a theory of truth, philosophy has no claim to privileged status among our discourses and projects. Ontological, epistemological, or ethical proposals would be just proposals to adopt favored construals.

PLATONIC CORRESPONDENCE

The first difficulty in Rorty's critique of correspondism is that correspondism and the correspondence theory of truth are not clear and monolithic enough to be neatly identified and described. In Rorty's work there is abundant characterization of correspondism and an underlying theory, but there are no alternative characterizations. Rorty assumes that, as a philosopher's invention, the correspondence theory of truth is singular and easily characterized. In both *Mirror* and *Consequences* Rorty construes correspondism as exhausted by a "faithful portrayal" theory that considers sentences and beliefs true by virtue of correspondence if they are deemed to accurately reflect, or replicate, facts.[1] Let me call this "Platonic" correspondism, to distinguish it from possible alternatives. Platonic correspondence is at the heart of Rorty's mirror imagery. Rorty identifies the misconception on which traditional epistemology is based: that truth is an accurate reflection, by particular thoughts or sentences, of particular facts. According to Rorty, knowledge as the general mirroring of nature—and the mind as the mirror—is the metaphor which has dominated philosophy since Plato. Consequently, in *Philosophy and the Mirror of Nature*, "Truth Without Mirrors" is the title of the section in chapter 6 in which Rorty considers truth, and chapter 8, the endorsement of hermeneutics, is titled "Philosophy Without Mirrors." It is of interest that Nietzsche anticipated Rorty's imagery:

> When we try to examine the mirror in itself we discover . . . nothing but things upon it. If we want to grasp the things we . . . get hold of nothing but the mirror.—This . . . is the history of knowledge.[2]

Nietzsche's point is deeper and perhaps subtler than Rorty's. As I indicated in the previous chapter, Nietzsche contends that the history of "knowledge," or epistemology in particular, has been a series of misconceptions about the mind and its objects. Rorty and Nietzsche agree that we inevitably reify the mind or its objects in philosophizing about knowledge. Rorty's concern is that traditional philosophy has reified mind into an epistemic mirror, which can only be what it is and do what it does if it reflects reality. Once that reification occurs, all the familiar problems follow about the nature of the mind and how it relates to the body, about how the mind reflects reality, and—most worrisome—about how we can know the mirroring is *accurate*. The long section in *Mirror* on the antipodeans, which many consider irrelevant or at least vastly overdone, aims in part to recall the knots we tie ourselves into when we predicate mental states as the necessary explanatory constituents of internal mirroring.

Rorty's main concern with truth in *Mirror* and *Consequences* is to expose the misconceived nature of truth as ideational and sentential replication of reality. There he gives a genealogical account of the mirror imagery of truth and reveals its incoherence. In "Pragmatism, Davidson and Truth," Rorty puts aside the metaphors of mirror imagery and discusses correspondism in terms of the idea that sentences are *made* true by correspondence to reality.[3] In both cases the goal is to deny that sentences or beliefs are true in virtue of some *property* that true sentences and beliefs share, and false sentences and beliefs lack, and that makes beliefs and sentences true in some constitutive way. This parallels the way Descartes thought of existence as a constitutive property of the actual. But in spite of the change of focus, Rorty's critique is still directed at a relational property of (accurate) correspondence of beliefs and sentences to the facts that constitute the object-referents of those beliefs and sentences.

In arguing against the admittedly correspondist philosophical tradition, Rorty makes a mistake something like the one he ascribes to philosophers since Kant. That is, he construes the tradition "Whiggishly," seeing it as dominated by a single conception of correspondism. Rorty structures his critique to approach correspondence from a number of directions, attempting always to exhibit both how it permeates the philosophic tradition and how it is simply unworkable. But his target is invariably a single theory. In this he is oddly indifferent to his own historicist message. While his objections to Plato's or Descartes's conceptions of truth are astute, it is questionable whether the views of, say, Aristotle would be as vulnerable to those objections.

To make his case against the correspondist philosophical tradition, Rorty would have to show that it is characterized by Platonic correspondism. And I think he would also have to demonstrate that Platonic correspondism does not underlie the mundane, nonphilosophical notion of truth. Otherwise, Rorty could not contrast ordinary uses of "true" with a theory-laden philosophical sense.

Rorty maintains that the ordinary uses of "true" do not entail or require a theoretically articulable notion of correspondence: correspondence is invented by philosophers to explain what needs no explanation. But it is here that his position becomes most implausible, because the philosophical account of correspondence—at least in its most general formulation—does not seem as distant from the ordinary notion of truth as Rorty suggests. That ordinary notion seems to turn, as Davidson has observed, on *some* sort of correspondence.

In place of corespondence, Rorty offers only linguistic practice and intralinguistic criteria, while we feel that our uses of "true" involve more. If something like Davidson's "correspondence from coherence" view does justice to those uses of truth, then Rorty's critique would be shown to focus on a particular—and extreme—interpretation of correspondence. Not only could we then try to articulate a viable interpretation of correspondence, we would also have to consider which figures in the tradition Rorty criticizes espouse Platonic correspondism, as opposed to other versions. And to the extent that the history displays a variety of correspondist views, Rorty's broader critique of the philosophical tradition would lose a great deal of force. For this reason I think it important to clarify at the outset Rorty's reading of correspondism as Platonic correspondism.

Having said the foregoing, I must add that it is wrong to think Rorty is attacking a strawman—a simplistic "picture theory" that no one would now take seriously. In spite of Dewey, Wittgenstein, and others, many philosophers still hold there are basic truths that provide us with starting points for philosophizing, and these truths are invariably described as cases wherein simple sentences describe evident facts. These may be perceptual or axiological, but they are held to be undeniable. The model here might be G. E. Moore's claim that observation of his own hands in front of his face was undeniable. Denial of the evident truth of such simple remarks will be dismissed as relativism or dubious epistemologizing. This view is no strawman. It expresses the conviction that some sentences do capture how things are, when the situations are simple and evident. The trouble is that the view is open to interpretations ranging from unworkable "picture" theories to innocuous positions, and that makes the appeal to evidency problematic, as it is not clear what epistemological and linguistic implications it carries. The view also begs the question by assuming that simple cases of description ("The cup is on the table") are unproblematic and involve little or no interpretation. Wilfrid Sellars taught us that it is a serious conceptual error to confuse the apparently simple with the elemental. "Red patch here, now" is as complex, in terms of conceptualization, as "There are neutrinos." "The cup is on the table," said while staring fixedly at the cup in question, is not a sentence—or belief—that somehow breaks through the skin of language or belief to provide an instance of unproblematic correspondence as a case of elemental description.

But the view in question is not altogether misconceived, for we seem to require *some* interpretation of correspondence to make sense of what we ordinarily say about truth and the world. For one thing, the view at issue is readily intelligible in a way that its denial is not. This may be only because of cognitive momentum, but it is something to be considered. We may be able to see the misconceived nature of Platonic correspondism, but we seem unable to abandon correspondence altogether and still make sense of language and the world as we understand them. This combination of ability and inability makes us feel Rorty is disingenuous in denying his views are relativistic, and evokes sympathy for Davidson's views on truth and realism.

THE REJECTION OF CORRESPONDISM

It is possible to begin a consideration of the nonpragmatic philosophers with a formulation of their main theses. Though it might simplify a given position, such a statement can serve as an orientation, if not as a summation. With pragmatists, the essentially critical nature of their views to a large extent precludes statements of this sort. Whereas one can say what most philosophers are *for*, one can best say what pragmatists are *against*.

But even in stating what they oppose, one must be careful not to characterize pragmatists—certainly neither Rorty nor Dewey—as critics within the philosophical tradition. The point is they are critics of that tradition itself. To describe Rorty's work as mainly a polemic against the correspondence theory of truth, for instance, is to risk the error so many of his critics make, which is to construe his as an alternative position which entails a competing philosophical theory. This is the mistake Meynell makes: to claim Rorty offers a critique based on, or at least implying, an alternative theoretical position. As mentioned in the last chapter, what Rorty wants to do is change the subject; he wants to abandon theorizing about truth because we cannot ask ahistorical questions and so cannot look for a theory which will constitute an ahistorical answer to a philosophical question about truth. Theorizing about truth is a fruitless exercise:

> pragmatists think that the history of attempts to isolate the True . . . or to define the word "true" . . . supports their suspicion that there is no interesting work to be done in this area . . . . When they suggest that we not ask questions about the nature of truth . . . they do not invoke a theory about the nature of reality or knowledge or man which says "there is no such thing as Truth . . . ." Nor do they have a "relativistic" or "subjectivist" theory of Truth . . . . They would simply like to change the subject.[4]

Rorty says theorizing about truth is not only unproductive, but also prompted by a misconceived felt-need for Cartesian certainty at the heart of traditional epistemology. This explains why his polemic against correspondism cannot be a counterargument. History shows that arguments against the felt-need for Cartesian certainty are not effective; otherwise, Dewey's and James's work would have sufficed. Instead Rorty offers a persuasive, many-sided discussion designed to bring out the wrongness of that felt-need.

A paradigmatic instance of Rorty's efforts to persuade through clarification and provocative questioning occurs in the introduction to *Consequences*, where Rorty tries to articulate what the pragmatist sees as the fundamental confusion in correspondism. The passage is clearly not an argument for a competing thesis; it is an expression of mild frustration and an illumination of an obsession with an unworkable idea: truth as objective and capturable in language. Moreover, the idea is itself perceived as nothing less than a fundamental truth and a condition of philosophical and general discourse.

> For the pragmatist, the notion of "truth" as something "objective" is just a confusion between (I) Most of the world is as it is whatever we think about it . . . and (II) There is something . . . called "the truth about the world" . . . . The pragmatist wholeheartedly assents to (I) . . . and cannot make any sense of (II). When the realist tries to explain (II) with (III) The truth about the world consists in a relation of "correspondence" between certain sentences . . . and the world itself, the pragmatist can only fall back on saying, once again, that many centuries of attempts to explain what "correspondence" is have failed . . . .[5]

Rorty rejects correspondence as a viable philosophical explanatory principle, not on the basis of counterarguments, but as a result of observation of the notion's abject failure and our manifest inability to neutrally compare sentences and beliefs to their objects. The notion at issue has simply never been made out. No one has ever succeeded in saying what correspondence consists of in the sense required by conception of correspondence as an explanatory principle. Correspondence remains a one-term "relation," like an analogy to something unknown. Perception and description of what a sentence allegedly corresponds to is always the possession or acquisition of belief and the use of language. The comparison required by correspondence for verification must always escape us, for we cannot make it except from within language and belief. But that is not to say that the failure of correspondence as an explanatory principle makes the world problematic.

Rorty alleges that there is no need for a theoretical explanation of how we say the world is as it is in terms of something *else*, namely, correspondence. The appeal to correspondence has never been more than an appeal to intuitive recognition of the point Hacking makes in discussing Davidson's "correspondence from coherence" view, which is that language as a whole corresponds to the world. But Rorty does not want to say even that much. Even if he granted the point, perhaps as an innocuous way of saying that we can cope with how things are, he would question the need to make the point at all because of the danger that it retains too much philosophical baggage from (Platonic) correspondence. In fact, Rorty's rejection of philosophy as a productive enterprise prevents him from accepting Davidson's view as a properly philosophical interpretation of correspondence. Rorty's identification of correspondence with Platonic correspondence means that nothing can be both an account of truth as correspondence and a viable position. This is why Rorty must construe Davidson as a pragmatist, albeit an unwilling or somewhat deluded one.

With respect to what *can* be said about truth—aside from philosophically uninteresting clarifications—Rorty limits discussion to intralinguistic considerations. Academic discussion of truth must be essentially clarificatory; either it can clarify specific practices, or it can be abstract and clarify the (actual) nature of language. For instance, regarding Tarski's semantic theory of truth, Rorty tells us that

> The pragmatist agrees with Davidson that to define such a predicate ["true"]—to develop a truth-theory for the sentences of English, e.g.,—would be a good way . . . to exhibit a natural language as a learnable, recursive structure, and thus give a systematic theory of meaning for the language. But he agrees with Davidson that such an exhibition is *all* that Tarski can give us, and all that can be milked out of Philosophical reflection on Truth.[6]

Tarski provides a way of understanding what we mean when we say a sentence is true, but that does not give a theoretical account of correspondence. To say "'Snow is white' is true if and only if snow is white" is to say under what conditions we count the sentence as true. However, the way those conditions are taken as established is a matter of perception and belief and, of course, the use of language. Rorty is anxious for us to see that no one could ever successfully say what it is for the sentence "Snow is white" to "correspond" to the brute whiteness of snow. And this is the key to his attack on correspondism.

Rorty attempts to provide neither arguments against a position nor alternatives to it, because he refuses to accept that there is a position to argue against. Correspondism can be a position only if (Platonic) correspondence is an intelligible notion capable of assessment. Rorty's claim is, in effect, that the notion is not intelligible. It only seems intelligible because many read Tarski's formulation, or something like it, as saying what it cannot say, namely, how a sentence relates to something outside language. Recognition that truth can only be amplified within language is the reason for replacing the notion of truth with one like warranted assertibility. The point is to introduce a notion which more clearly shows how "is true" has a commendatory role, how its use acknowledges that articulation of a particular sentence is a sanctioned move in a language game.

Once we recognize the intralinguistic nature of truth, we realize how correspondence is, in any case, fruitless. As an alleged theoretical account of how sentences relate to the world, correspondence gets us nowhere at all with respect to what really interests us. As Rorty says in speaking of James's views on truth,

> it is the vocabulary of practise rather than of theory, of action rather than contemplation, in which one can say something useful about truth. Nobody engages in epistemology or semantics because he wants to know how "This is red" pictures the world. Rather, we want to know in what sense Pasteur's views of disease picture the world accurately and Paracelsus' inaccurately, or what exactly . . . Marx pictured more accurately than Machiavelli. But just here the vocabulary of "picturing" fails us.[7]

The picturing vocabulary fails us because there is no linguistic portrayal. Language simply does not work that way, nor could we tell if it did. We use language to articulate constructions we impose, ways of construing situations. Part of the force of James's notion that truth is what works is that our concern with truth is, as this passage suggests, a concern with whether a certain construction gets us what we want or hangs together well with others that do. The bad philosophical move is to try to explain successful constructions and impositions in terms of faithful ideational or linguistic reproductions.

It may be useful to note at this point that the wrongness of the notion that true sentences are somehow reproductions has been stressed by Gadamer in his philosophical hermeneutics. Gadamer is especially concerned that interpretation not be conceived as the achievement of true sentences which reproduce the determinate, intended thoughts of an author or speaker. Understanding another, or a text, is for Gadamer a complex process of anticipation of meaning and of change in oneself, for understanding, as a (Heideggerian) form of being, is always conditioned by its objects. To understand a text or a speaker is to achieve a "fusion of horizons" in which there can be no simplistic talk about truth as accuracy of reproduction. Gadamer rejects the notion that there is such a thing as *correct* interpretation, that is, interpretation which is faithful to the thought and intention of an author or a speaker. More generally, Gadamer expounds an historicist view of truth, in which truth is not, and cannot be, an accurate rendition of something determinate, but is instead a kind of validated consensus. Unlike North American philosophers concerned with truth, however, Gadamer rarely deals with *descriptive* truth, or sentences which are true descriptions of states of affairs. His focus is always on communicated ideas, and especially our appropriation of ideas from distant times or from different cultures. This focus explains part of Rorty's interest in hermeneutics, for Gadamer is concerned with understanding others, not with boring questions about accurate sentential rendition of cats-on-mats. In this way hermeneutics is already postphilosophical in Rorty's sense, for its problems are problems about human understanding and relations, not Cartesian puzzles about "external reality."

Rorty's brief discussion of Gadamer in chapter 8 of *Mirror* begins by characterizing philosophical hermeneutics as a rejection of the "classic" conception of human beings as having an essential need and capacity to capture essences, or, in more Aristotelian terms, to know truth. Rorty lauds Gadamer for his forceful reminder that " . . . we need a sense of the relativity of descriptive vocabularies to periods, traditions, and historical accidents," and hence that there can be no apprehension of ahistorical truth as the essence of coming to know.[8]

Rorty's discussion of Gadamer is less concerned with truth than with making out his own idea of edifying philosophy, of philosophy that is "abnormal." (Recall Thomas Kuhn's notion of revolutionary science as "abnormal" science.) What Rorty says here about truth is summarized in his comment that objective truth "is no more and no less than the best idea we currently have about how to explain what is going on."[9] As for Gadamer's views on truth, it is noteworthy that he also succumbs to mirror imagery:

> . . . in the last analysis language is not simply a mirror. What we perceive in it is not merely a "reflection" of our own and all being; it is the living out of . . . all the other relationships and dependencies that comprise our world.[10]

As noted, Gadamer's remarks reflect his conception of language as the medium of our being and the Heideggerian notion that understanding is a mode of being, not the acquisition of propositions. But mirror imagery and ontological turns notwithstanding, what is significant here is that, like Rorty, Gadamer leaves us with a deep ambiguity regarding truth.

Bernstein describes Gadamer's view of truth as one of "communicative understanding," but notes that there is in the exposition of that view a real danger of relativism.[11] The basic problem is that of *validation*, which supposedly occurs in spite of all the objections to correspondist thinking, but which is never really construed as anything *more* than agreement.

In Gadamer's *Truth and Method*—which contains remarkably little of what North American philosophers would consider discussion of truth—we read that "True historical thinking must take account of its own historicality." This suggests that there is some way to get past, or allow for, our "prejudgments" or "prejudices" or anticipations of meaning and significance.[12] The implication here is that validation is achieved, that there is in consensus more than *just* agreement. This idea recalls one I will consider in connection with Dewey, namely, Peirce's rather unpragmatic trust in progress in inquiry. But Gadamer's book concludes with the claim that "there is . . . no understanding that is free of all prejudices . . . ."[13] So we are left feeling that, however much "fusing of horizons" occurs, however productive our appropriation of points of view, and however successful our anticipation of meaning in understanding texts and other speakers, we never achieve more than what might be only our own subjective construals.

Like Rorty, Gadamer rejects the notion that truth is the adequacy of thoughts or sentences to "the facts" as simplistic and a product of the traditional philosophical need for certainty. But he does not see his own historicist conception of truth as relativistic. Again like Rorty, Gadamer baffles us with his conviction that he is not denying *truth*, only a hopeless misconception of it as ahistorical and capable of accurate portrayal. Both appeal to communicative understanding and consensus as the crucial (intralinguistic) criterion for correctness, but both deny that they thereby make truth or validation relative to social or psychological factors. They try to convince us that our demand for greater clarity regarding the nature of truth, for a clear repudiation or preclusion of relativism, results from a misconceived application of the traditional dichotomies between the epistemologically certain and the problematic, between truth as correspondence and as mere coherence, between knowledge and opinion.

Rorty tries to engage the foregoing issue by distinguishing between ordinary and theoretical characterizations of truth. He attempts to illustrate how philosophical worries about truth and relativism arise only if we retain the unworkable theoretical machinery of the Plato-Descartes-Kant tradition.

Rorty tries to discern a difference between innocent and tendentious understandings of correspondence in order to protect unphilosophical beliefs and practices concerning truth. When we say a sentence states the facts or corresponds to the facts—both perfectly acceptable phrases—we are supposedly not talking about *philosophical* correspondence, and hence should raise no worrisome issues. Rorty here recalls David Hume, who charged that the distinction between perceptions and their objects was a philosophical creation attributable to those who, like Descartes and John Locke, read their epistemological suppositions into the "vulgar" person's practices. And just as Locke's distinction between perceptions and their objects was shown to be unworkable by George Berkeley and Hume, Rorty is trying to demonstrate that the notion of correspondence becomes unviable when it is pushed beyond the ordinary things we say about truth. If there is to be discussion of truth, it must be intralinguistic clarification of our practices. If that seems inadequate, the fault is in our expectations, not in language or the world. The trouble is that, as with Hume's project, we feel that the defense of the vulgar is costing us a crucial distinction. In the case of Hume we are left with only impressions and ideas, while in the case of Rorty we feel we are left with only our beliefs and construals.

The important point here that cannot be denied or overlooked is that truth-as-correspondence does not name a special *property*. Consider that it is not completely vacuous to say that opium puts one to sleep because it has a dormative power. This says at least that opium is the operant agent in causing sleep because of certain unspecified properties. The remark is almost vacuous because we want to know more, namely, what those properties are. Saying that "Snow is white" is true if and only if snow is white is like saying that opium has a dormative power. It tells us something obvious. But unlike the opium remark, the remark about truth neither says nor implies anything about the supposed "property" of correspondence that makes the sentence true. A true sentence will not yield to analysis some property that makes it true, as an analysis of opium will yield details about its dormative power. The pragmatist, Rorty claims, is impatient with theorizing about correspondence because she does not see that anything is added to what we ordinarily say about sentences being true, by saying that they are true in virtue of correspondence. Correspondence does not name a property that, when present, makes sentences true.

But the denial that correspondence is a property, which most would take as unproblematic, falls somewhat short of the pragmatist's real claim. And this is where we find some ambiguity in Rorty's position. He often sounds as if it would suffice that correspondence not be thought a property, and hence not be laden with philosophical theory, but be left instead to function in its mundane sense, as when we say that a sentence or description corresponds to the facts. But at other times it seems the notion of correspondence must be *unintelligible* in all its manifestations, as if there is no mundane sense. If in fact the pragmatist understood the notion of correspondence, it would be absurd to say that truth is what works or what is warrantedly assertible. That would be like the materialist accepting the distinction between mind and body as viable and then arguing that there is body only. The materialist must argue that there is neither need for, nor possibility of, making an ontological distinction between mind and body. In a similar way, the pragmatist must reject the notion of correspondence as unintelligible, instead of trying to make it out to be something else or denying that it is a property. In this sense pragmatism is an antimetaphysical position, and correspondism, at least the Platonic variety, is a metaphysical view which casts language and belief as a phenomenal realm, the world as a noumenal realm, and "hard" reference as the impossible link between them. Alternatively, one can describe pragmatism as antiessentialist, as denying that there is *anything* in virtue of which sentences are true, including some nonproperty relation of correspondence which has perhaps not yet been made clear, such as Davidson's.

The reality sentences describe serves as provenance just in being described, but pragmatism cannot allow that reality to thereby enter into a relation of correspondence with those sentences. As I will say in the next section, sentences can only be so many more bits of reality. However, if reality does not collaborate with language in making sentences true, neither is it jeopardized by failing to do so. The world is as it is whatever we think or say about it. We are unfortunately plagued by the idea that we enter into a more intimate relation with it when we manage to describe it correctly, when we capture it in language. This leads us to think that our language is, and must be, anchored in the world; that it "hooks up" to the world just where true descriptive sentences "correspond to the facts." And this encourages many to think that the denial of correspondence must be either an espousal of idealism or the acceptance that there is no "objective" reality beyond that of our beliefs.

What we have so far might be glossed as follows: according to Rorty the correspondist philosophical tradition is based on a bad promissory note; the notion that sentences are true because they "correspond" to reality has never been demonstrated. If we look at what actually goes on, we find that questions about truth are productive and intelligible only when they are about what we say and do according to linguistic criteria and practices. Nonetheless, we must acknowledge that even though we cannot approach it through certain privileged-status sentences, there is a brute reality that underlies what we say and do. The mistake is to try to weave that reality into what we say and believe by making it an epistemic component of our sayings and beliefs, that is, the "correspondence" to reality of those sayings and beliefs. But it is also a mistake to take more than passing notice of brute reality. Trying to say more about it, as when one attempts to counter skepticism, can only generate epistemologizing and hence bad philosophy.

PRESERVING REALITY

In "Texts and Lumps," a piece written recently, we find a passage that echoes assertions in *Consequences* that we are able to establish a kind of correspondence between sentences, as bits of the world, and things or events, as other bits of the world. Rorty tells us that

> Pragmatists say that the traditional notion that "truth is correspondence to reality" is an uncashable and outworn metaphor. Some true statements—like "The cat is on the mat"—can be paired off with hunks of reality so as to associate parts of the statement with parts of the chosen chunk. Most true statements—like "The cat is *not* on the mat" and "There are transfinite numbers" and "Pleasure is better than pain"—cannot. Furthermore, we will be no better off even if we construct a metaphysical scheme which pairs off something in the world with all parts of *every* true statement . . . . For we should still be faced with the question of whether the . . . language we use *itself* "corresponds to reality." That is, we should still wonder whether talk of cats or numbers or goodness is the right way to break up the universe into chunks, whether our language cuts reality at the joints. The pragmatists conclude that the intuition that truth is correspondence should be extirpated rather than explicated.[14]

This passage is similar to several others in Rorty's recent papers and books.[15] I want to stress here Rorty's conviction that whatever there is to the correspondence "intuition" can be explained and understood in terms of our ability to "pair off" bits of language, as bits of the world, with other bits of the world, but that once we go beyond the most elementary pairings, correspondence ceases to be intelligible. In short, the philosophical notion of correspondence results from fallacious thinking: taking a few examplary cases—where pairing works—as evidence of something fundamental in the relation of language to the world.

Rorty has another conviction, namely, that if correspondence is allowed as a viable philosophical notion, we will be trapped into conceptual-scheme relativism. This is the main reason he sees Davidson's arguments against the scheme/content distinction as consistent with the pragmatic rejection of correspondence. I think the connection is as follows: as the above passage notes, even if the correspondence view were made out, we would wonder if language as a whole correctly portrays the world. That is, if individual sentences are true because of "correspondence," is the whole of language true in the same way, and is there a determinate reality which might be "cut up" in different ways by varying conceptual schemes? If so, there would be a real question as to whether our particular conceptual scheme was the *right* one. But as there is no conceivable way of establishing the correspondence of the whole of language to the world, we would have to acquiesce in a fruitless and philosophically stultifying relativism. In this way Rorty is as much an antirelativist as anyone.[16]

While not prepared to offer a positive theory of truth, Rorty does feel obliged to say something more about reality because, as has been indicated, construing truth as intralinguistic seems to jeopardize factuality. Rorty answers that the pragmatist, when told that there are hard facts to account for, notes a shift from truth to factuality and then "construes the reputed hardness of facts as an artifact produced by our choice of language-game."[17] Having explained truth in terms of linguistic practices, the pragmatist acknowledges factuality as a brute reality that, while continuous with those practices, does not constitute an epistemic component of them.

The nonpragmatist argues that rejection of correspondence implies the denial of factuality as a standard for belief and description. And this is correct, for Rorty is denying access to an extralinguistic *standard* to which sentences conform. But for the nonpragmatist, the denial jeopardizes factuality itself—or at least renders it unknowable. Nor is Rorty's answer reassuring, for he describes the hardness of facts as "simply the hardness of the previous agreements within a community about the consequences of a certain event."[18] Rorty's position will resemble idealism or some form of phenomenalism. He is conscious of this danger and disavows idealism, but does not explicitly endorse realism. He tries to dismiss both the charge of idealism and the entire debate by impugning their enabling conditions.

Rorty concurs with the nonpragmatist who argues that nothing about linguistic conventions or conceptualization alters either reality or some of the data it produces, but he thinks the nonpragmatist moves illegitimately from this fact to the philosophical tenet that reality must be accessible in its unaffected state. When sentences are taken to correspond to reality, that reality is thought to be captured in its unaffected state. It is with reference to these alleged paradigms of correspondence that Rorty admits we can pair some sentences with reality, such as "The cat is on the mat" with a cat on a mat, and then be tempted to think we understand correspondence. However, when we consider sentences like "The cat is *not* on the mat," we either realize that correspondence does not work, or begin producing elaborate and unworkable philosophical devices, such as "negative facts." Rorty does not deny factuality. He denies that brute reality somehow enters language as a *relatum* in correspondence, or, conversely, that correspondence provides a way out of language to the world. When the nonpragmatist raises the matter of brute reality,

> the pragmatist meets this point by differentiating himself from the idealist. He agrees that there is such a thing as brute physical resistance—the pressure of light waves on Galileo's eyeball, or of the stone on Dr. Johnson's boot. But [the pragmatist] sees no way of transferring this nonlinguistic brutality to . . . the truth of sentences.[19]

Rorty describes facts as hybrid entities, saying that the causes of the assertibility of sentences "include both physical stimuli and our antecedent choice of response to such stimuli."[20] But once factuality has made its necessary contribution, conceptualization and language take over. Rorty denies the possibility of comparing items in consciousness to brute reality through "correspondence." But that is not to deny that those items are products of brute reality.

The trouble with the foregoing is that most will feel that, in spite of everything said, Rorty can only postulate brute reality; that without correspondence he cannot prevent his position from being idealistic or phenomenalistic—or at best "possibilistic," as is Descartes's position regarding extended matter prior to the sixth *Meditation*. The problem is that in Rorty's pragmatic view language nowhere hooks up to reality. There are no "basic" sentences that serve as anchors for the whole of language. The nonpragmatist will see as empty Rorty's acknowledgment that the world is as it is, since Rorty can provide no cases where it is certainly so described. Pairing up sentences and simple situations cannot serve as cases of true description in the correspondist sense, because the whole point is that Rorty treats both sentences and situations as bits of the world. His pairings are too much like mere juxtapositions of objects. Nothing follows. The nonpragmatist demands at least one case where "pairing" is *true description*. Rorty cannot allow true description, because his position is precisely that "correspondence" cannot be made out in the sense of saying when a descriptive sentence matches what it describes.

Nonetheless, Rorty does not open a gap between us and language on the one hand, and the world on the other. Unlike the skeptic, he does not distance us as conscious, language-using entities from "external" reality. Rorty thinks that we reach the world all the time, as when we pair a sentence with some part of it. What he disallows is that such pairing is or can amount to a *comparing* of sentences and the world. He denies that we can sometimes take a position at right angles to both language and the world, thus enabling us to judge how the two relate to one another. The skeptic sets the problem by opening up the epistemic gap between perception and its objects. The correspondist accepts the existence of this gap and maintains that it is crossed by reference and correspondence: that is, at least some of our sentences "connect" with what is on the other side of the epistemic gap, and thus enable us to anchor ourselves in the "objectively" real. When Rorty rejects correspondism, he also rejects the gap.

Rorty's is, as many have observed, a "deconstructive" critique. He maintains that if the correspondist construes the relation of sentences to the world as one of "correspondence," and if correspondence is the way we cross the epistemic gap, then the correspondist's own presuppositions make correspondence an unintelligible notion. Once the epistemic gap is even tacitly accepted, *nothing could possibly count* as correspondence. Talk of correspondence can be viable only as long as it is not theoretical, that is, if it is limited to the sort of mundane things we say when we describe sentences as true or as stating the facts. A philosophical account of the mundane things we say can only be a kind of amplification of the intralinguistic criteria we use for saying that a sentence is true, and of the practices we engage in when we assess what people say.

Rorty preserves reality or avoids idealism, then, by disallowing philosophical discussion of reality. In the next chapter I will explore this point more carefully, when I consider Rorty's resistance to Davidson's acceptance of the realist/nonrealist debate as a serious one—an acceptance that jeopardizes Davidson's putative pragmatism. But before comparing Rorty to his contemporary Davidson, I want to devote the balance of this chapter to some remarks about Rorty's relation to Dewey.

RORTY AND DEWEY

I think it is a mistake to claim Rorty exalts Dewey because his own views on truth are derived from Dewey's, or because Rorty's own pragmatism derives from that of Dewey. Rorty's relation to Dewey is more complex. First, Dewey is more an example of someone holding Rorty's views on the bankruptcy of theorizing about truth, than he is an intellectual forebear. Dewey exemplifies the turning away from a foundationalist, correspondist philosophical tradition, which Rorty sees as prelude to a postphilosophical age. There is no *doctrinal* connection between Dewey and Rorty, in spite of the coincidence of many of their views. Second, Rorty considers Dewey an external critic of the philosophical tradition, unique in the way Wittgenstein was unique. It is crucial to Rorty's notion of an "edifying" philosophy, which Dewey's is, that Dewey does not have doctrinal followers, that he is not the founder of an alternative philosophical tradition of which Rorty could be a member. Rorty sees himself as an external critic and, modesty aside, places himself in the "edifying" tradition of Wittgenstein, Heidegger, and Dewey.

Rorty lists Dewey, with Wittgenstein and Heidegger, as one of "the three most important philosophers of our century."[21] It might seem problematic that it is Dewey, not James, whom Rorty chooses, since he refers to James in various discussions of truth. But Rorty values Dewey's general stance more than that of James, which was less radical than Dewey's rejection of the entire tradition, backed up with productive contributions to culture in practical areas. There is a fairly clear sense in which James is still doing philosophy, even though as a pragmatist. Dewey's views were inspirational for Rorty, rather than methodologically influential, as were those of Richard McKeon and Robert Brumbaugh,

whom Rorty mentions in the Preface to *Mirror,* or intellectually stimulat-
ing, as were those of Davidson, or complementary, as were those of Quine
or Sellars. Rorty has built on the work of Sellars and Quine, and if he has
developed anyone's views, he has developed Davidson's—as he has ad-
mitted in conversation. He no doubt owes intellectual debts to his teachers. But Dewey offered a *model*—a model of what should follow philosophy.

Dewey eschewed correspondism, more as a consequence of his views on
experience and inquiry than as a deliberate rejection of the correspondence theory as such. He was not offering an alternative account of truth
in the way that James and Peirce at least approached. What he says about
truth results from a different vision of human consciousness. Dewey
thought the philosophical tradition was all wrong, as Heidegger and
Wittgenstein later did. He could not offer putatively better theories within
the confines of that tradition. In this way Dewey stepped outside of
philosophy, and Rorty is a "Deweyan" only in the sense that he takes
Dewey as an inspirational figure, as an edifying philosopher. Rorty could
not set about "developing" Dewey's views on truth or pragmatism without violating both his own principles and Dewey's. To better understand
the connection between the two, one has to note the generality of Rorty's
remarks about Dewey. There are no appeals to Dewey as an authority on
pragmatism, though there are quotes illustrating his pragmatism. One
finds instead broad references to Dewey's vision. Even where Rorty is
concerned with specific points of comparison between Dewey and Heidegger, and where he considers Dewey's inclination to metaphysics, the
references to Dewey are not defensive explanations and amplifications of
the work of a predecessor. They are references designed to bring out the
integrity and radicalness of Dewey's vision.[22]

In the introduction to *Mirror,* Rorty correctly states that Dewey rejected
foundationalism. But he stresses that this rejection occurred in the context
of a holistic vision of what human intellectual and practical life should be.

> Dewey . . . wrote his polemics against traditional mirror-imagery out
> of a vision of a new kind of society. In his ideal society, culture is no
> longer dominated by the ideal of objective cognition but by that of
> aesthetic enhancement.[23]

Rorty considers Dewey a precursor and prophet of the postphilosophical society. Dewey earns his elevated place as one of the three most

important philosophers of our time by encouraging us to "put aside that spirit of *seriousness* which artists traditionally lack and philosophers are traditionally supposed to maintain."[24] Even in the one discussion that approaches an apology, wherein Rorty tries to excuse Dewey's early metaphysical ambitions, Dewey is portrayed as deconstructing philosophy as the later Wittgenstein did:

> [Dewey] wanted to sketch a culture that would not continually give rise to new versions of the old problems, because it would no longer make the distinctions between Truth, Goodness, and Beauty which engender such problems. . . . In doing this larger job, his chief enemy was the notion of Truth as accuracy of representation . . . Dewey thought that if he could break down this notion, if scientific inquiry could be seen as adapting and coping rather than copying, the continuity between science, morals, and art would become apparent.[25]

As Rorty reads Dewey, the slow development from a fascination with metaphysics to paradigmatic pragmatism was comparable to the ways Wittgenstein and Heidegger changed their philosophical positions and repudiated the presuppositions that informed their early work. In the essay comparing Heidegger and Dewey, Rorty contrasts Dewey with Heidegger by stressing the former's turn away from philosophy, his rejection of philosophy as a particular activity. The burden of the characterization is that Dewey, like Rorty, saw the vacuity and inherent danger in capital-P Philosophy. In this way, Dewey was more like the later Wittgenstein than like Heidegger, who alone among the three maintained an embarrassing commitment to philosophy as something *special* in which *progress* might be made. Dewey did turn away from philosophy; he exemplified Rorty's postphilosophic person. That turning away is clearest in the dismissal of epistemology. In what some consider Dewey's most mature work, *Logic: The Theory of Inquiry*, published in 1938, we read that

> A more detailed examination would confirm the point that has been made more than once, namely, that epistemology, so called, is a mixture of logical conceptions, derived from analysis of competent inquiry, and irrelevant psychological and metaphysical preconceptions.[26]

This statement comes some nine years after Dewey's criticism, in *Experience and Nature* (1929), of traditional rationalism and empiricism, during which he tells us that the test of "the value of any philosophy" is simply "Does it end in conclusions which, when . . . referred back to ordinary life-experiences . . . render them more significant, more luminous to us, and make our dealings with them more fruitful?"[27] This view is echoed in the preface to *Logic*, when Dewey considers the term "pragmatism" and says its "proper interpretation" refers to "consequences as necessary tests of the validity of propositions . . . ."[28] It is in this sense that Dewey characterizes his text as "thoroughly pragmatic."

Dewey not only rejects the philosophic tradition by deconstructing its core principles, he rejects it by denying philosophy's claim to ahistorical and abstract status. Philosophizing is worthwhile only if it has beneficial practical consequences; the problems it deals with should have useful analogues or applications. It is this spirit that Rorty applauds more than a particular view of truth or a particular characterization of pragmatism as an alternative philosophical methodology. In spite of the emphasis I put on Rorty's rejection of correspondism at the beginning of this chapter, it must be remembered that truth-as-correspondence is only the main tool of what Rorty most wants to debunk: the conception of philosophy as the ahistorical adjudicator of reason. In the present context our focus is philosophical; if we were considering Rorty in a broader context, we would have to focus on what he construes as his central cultural contribution: putting philosophy in its place. The rejection of mirror-imagery or "copy" theories of truth and epistemology, of foundationalism, of the Kantian perception of philosophy as a single discipline with a 2500-year history, all reduce philosophy to another voice in "the conversation of mankind" and bring it down from its presumptuous—and self-ascribed—position as the judge of rationality. According to Rorty, Dewey tried to do just that. Therefore Dewey is an "edifying" philosopher, a revolutionary, an inspiration. To see Dewey as someone whose theses are to be developed or adapted would be to assimilate him into the tradition he repudiated. In a passage in *Mirror*, where Rorty acknowledges a methodological debt to Quine, Sellars, and Davidson, he speaks very differently of Dewey, as of Wittgenstein and Heidegger. He remarks that he is indebted to Quine and others for the means he employs, but his debt to Dewey is "for the ends to which these means are put."[29]

But having clarified how Rorty is not a "Deweyan," we should acknowledge that his reading of Dewey is somewhat selective. Rorty downplays what he finds in Dewey that is not to his liking, in particular,

Dewey's commitment to rational inquiry or "scientific method" in its broadest sense. In *Logic* Dewey makes only passing reference to truth, relying exclusively on his "warranted assertibility" formula. But it is significant that the only notable reference is in a footnote wherein he endorses Peirce's notion of truth as "concordance" at the end of inquiry.[30] Rorty at one point agreed with, but has since rejected, Peirce's notion.[31] The problem for Rorty has to do with what we might call Dewey's optimism. To refer again to *Logic*, Dewey does endorse Peirce's definition of truth as "The opinion which is fated to be ultimately agreed to by all who investigate,"[32] and he ends *Logic* with a ringing statement on the nature of inquiry:

> Since scientific methods simply exhibit free intelligence operating in the best manner available at a given time, the cultural waste, confusion and distortion that results from the failure to use these methods, in all fields in connection with all problems, is incalculable. These considerations reinforce the claim of logical theory, as the theory of inquiry, to assume and to hold a position of primary human importance.[33]

Dewey's notion of inquiry is one of *determination*. We are told that "Inquiry is the directed or controlled transformation of an indeterminate situation into a determinately unified one."[34] The process is one of imaginative anticipation and invention of solutions and productive construals, and of observation and imposition. And while none of this clearly contradicts Rorty's views, aside from the nod of Peirce, there is some question as to how Rorty can account for Dewey's methodological optimism. The whole of *Logic* is devoted to articulating the problems and procedures of logical inquiry or scientific method in a way that definitively separates that method from other discourses, and as definitively assigns to it responsibilities and—most important—advantages and promise beyond other discourses. This discrepancy between Dewey and Rorty underscores the problems that Rorty has in trying to construe science as just another discourse. In chapter 4 I will consider this question more fully in connection with an objection made by Bernard Williams to Rorty's view of the status of science.

To sum up my assessment of Rorty's relationship to Dewey, the salient point is that Rorty is an admirer of Dewey, not an expounder or disciple.

Rorty's view that truth is intralinguistic and should be understood in terms of language games or practices owes a great deal more to Wittgenstein than to Dewey. Furthermore, Dewey and Rorty differ markedly with respect to the status and nature of inquiry and of scientific method in particular. "Logical" or rigorously reasoned inquiry and science were not just so many more discourses for Dewey.

What I am stressing here is Rorty's hermeneutical approach. With respect to philosophers he finds inspiring, challenging, or simply interesting, Rorty's project is never to "get them right" in the sense of aiming at a *correct* interpretation. He does not believe such a correct interpretation is any more possible than does Gadamer. The project is always to see what ideas are most useful to us, in our time and given our objectives and history. Rorty tells us that " . . . a thinker's own self-image may not be usable by his heirs. . . . I am trying to adapt pragmatism to a changed intellectual environment . . . ."[35]

Some may consider Rorty's attitude irresponsible, and thereby draw attention to a dispute about interpretation or appropriation with illuminating parallels to the dispute over Rorty's alleged relativism. One can charge irresponsibility with respect to interpretation or appropriation of theses and ideas only if one assumes, against Gadamerian hermeneutical principles, that there exist both *what* an author meant and the possibility of readers discerning *just* what she or he meant. If one believes, as do Gadamer and Rorty, that all reading is interpreting, that all *understanding* is "tailored" appropriation, the charge of irresponsibility is an empty one. Nonetheless, we are left with doubts, as in the case of truth and relativism, for we feel that there must be restrictions on appropriation, while it is not clear how Rorty can allow them at all. What we find at this juncture is Rorty's profound trust in *reasonableness*, and it is appropriate to conclude this first look at his views on truth with one of Rorty's expressions of that trust. In "Science and Solidarity" Rorty tells us that

> Another meaning for "rational" is . . . something like "sane" or "reasonable" rather than "methodical." It names a set of moral virtues: tolerance, respect for the opinions of those around one, willingness to listen . . . [36]

Truth does not provide a standard for interpretation or anything else: we have no foolproof methodologies by which to proceed with confidence that we are getting things *right*. We can rely only on ourselves, and when we rely on ourselves in interpreting the work of another, we rely on a reasonableness that is itself defined by our practices and the responses and practices of our fellows. The real test for interpretation, given that it is reasonable, is how productive our readings are. When we consider our heroes and predecessors, we have our stories about the stories they told, just as our successors will have their stories about the stories we told.

I think Rorty would agree with Peter Jones that, however creative our interpretation, we can still attempt to put ourselves as much as possible into the epoch and mind-set of a given author, if our interest is not in appropriating but in understanding—as closely as we can—that author's own interpretation of her or his own work.[37] This is what scholars do, but it is not Rorty's interest in Dewey—or in Davidson, for that matter. Then there was Dewey. Now there is also Rorty's Dewey. The only issue is which we find most productive in our own projects.

The foregoing perhaps suffices with respect to Rorty's relation to Dewey. Of greater immediate philosophic interest are Rorty's contemporary critics and competitors. Davidson looms very large on the present philosophical scene, and Rorty's admiration and development of his work is evident. Rorty has tried to construe Davidson as a pragmatist, assimilating what he admires of Davidson's views on truth while distancing Davidson from commitments Rorty considers misconceived. In the next chapter I will look more closely at Rorty's views on truth, focusing on his efforts to read Davidson as a pragmatist—less to say something about Davidson than to say more about Rorty.

Notes

1. Often the characterization of correspondence includes reference or "hard" reference as the link between sentential replications and bits of the world. By "hard" reference I mean realistically conceived connections between sentences and events, objects, or juxtapositions of objects. The notion is clearest in the early Wittgenstein's picture-theory of meaning and in causal theories of reference. Perhaps the central point is that reference is not contingent on intention. See Rorty, *Consequences*, xxiii, and Rorty, *Mirror*, 293.
2. Friedrich Nietzsche, *Daybreak*, trans. R. J. Hollingdale (Cambridge: Cambridge University Press, 1982), par. 243, p. 141.
3. Rorty, "Pragmatism, Davidson and Truth," p. 5.
4. Rorty, *Consequences*, xiv.
5. Ibid., xxvi.
6. Ibid.

7. Ibid., 162.
8. Rorty, *Mirror*, 363.
9. Ibid., 385.
10. Hans-Georg Gadamer, *Philosophical Hermeneutics*, ed. and trans. David Linge (Berkeley and Los Angeles: University of California Press, 1976), 32.
11. Bernstein, *Beyond Objectivism*, 168.
12. Hans-Georg Gadamer, *Truth and Method*, ed. and trans. G. Barden and J. Cumming (New York: Seabury Press, 1975), 267.
13. Ibid., 446.
14. Richard Rorty, "Texts and Lumps," forthcoming in *New Literary History*, 4.
15. For example, in "Pragmatism, Relativism and Irrationalism," in *Consequences*, 162, we read:

> . . . one can, to be sure, pair off bits of the language with bits of what one takes the world to be in such a way that the sentences one believes true have internal structures isomorphic to relations between things in the world. When we rap out routine undeliberated reports like "This is water," "That's red," . . . our short categorical sentences can easily be thought of as pictures . . . . Such reports do indeed pair little bits of language with little bits of the world. Once one gets to negative universal hypotheticals, and the like, such pairing will become messy and *ad hoc* . . . .

See also 18 n. 13, and *Mirror*, 300.
16. Rorty's antirelativism is perhaps most evident in his dismissal of relativism in "Pragmatism, Relativism, and Irrationalism," *Consequences*, 166:

> "Relativism" is the view that every belief . . . is as good as every other. No one holds this view. Except for the occasional cooperative freshman, one cannot find anybody who says that two incompatible opinions on an important topic are equally good. The philosophers who get *called* "relativists" are those who say that the grounds for choosing between such opinions are less algorithmic than had been thought.

17. Rorty, "Texts and Lumps," 5.
18. Ibid.
19. Ibid., 6.
20. Ibid.
21. Rorty, *Mirror*, 5.
22. See Rorty, *Mirror*, 5–6, 9, 13, 162, 362n, 367–68, 381–82; and Rorty, *Consequences*, xvii–xix, xxiv–xxv, 12, 13–14, 28–29, 40, 43–47, 49–54, 73–75, 79, 84, 86, 127, 160–66, 174–75, 193, 203–08.

23. Rorty, *Mirror*, 13.
24. Rorty, *Consequences*, 87.
25. Ibid., 86.
26. John Dewey, *Logic: The Theory of Inquiry* (New York: Henry Holt, 1938), 525.
27. John Dewey, *Experience and Nature* (New York: Open Court, 1929), 6–8.
28. Dewey, *Logic*, iv.
29. Rorty, *Mirror*, 7. The passage reads as follows:

> ... most of the particular criticisms of the tradition which I offer are
> borrowed from such systematic philosophers as Sellars, Quine, David-
> son, Ryle, Malcolm, Kuhn, and Putnam. I am as much indebted to these
> philosophers for the means I employ as I am to Wittgenstein, Heidegger,
> and Dewey for the ends to which these means are put.

30. Dewey, *Logic*, 345n.
31. See, for example, Rorty, *Consequences*, 165, xlv n. 25; also Rorty, "Pragmatism,
    Davidson and Truth," 9–10, 10n.
32. Dewey, *Logic*, 345n.
33. Ibid., 535.
34. Ibid., 117.
35. In Rorty's exchange with John J. McDermott, R. W. Sleeper and Abraham
    Edel, "Symposium on Rorty's *Consequences of Pragmatism*," in *Transactions of the
    Charles S. Peirce Society* 21 (1985): 47. As in the case of Dewey, Rorty takes
    inspiration where he can. His John Milton Scott lecture, "Freud and Moral
    Reflection," given at Queen's University, Kingston, Ontario, on 23 January
    1986, made much of a rejection of the notion of a "core" self which Rorty
    attributed to Freud, to the discomfort of several Freudians in the audience.
36. Richard Rorty, "Science as Solidarity," read at McMaster University, Hamil-
    ton, Ontario, 20 January 1986, 3.
37. See Peter Jones, *Philosophy and the Novel* (Oxford: Oxford University Press,
    1975), chapter 5; see also my *Making Believe: Philosophical Reflections on Fiction*
    (London: Greenwood Press, 1984).

Chapter 3

Truth and the Redundancy of Realism

PRELIMINARY REMARKS

This chapter questions whether Rorty can scuttle philosophy by showing that the issue of truth is beset by misconceptions arising from the felt need for Cartesian certainty. I cannot hope to fully resolve this matter, but do intend to show that Rorty is at best optimistic in thinking he has dealt with the issue of truth. My argument is that the issue of truth will not evaporate, and that, as Davidson's theorizing illustrates, it admits of progress toward resolution. However, Rorty does not offer a competing theory of truth, so we cannot proceed by assessing the relative merits of the correspondence theory and one proposed by Rorty. Instead we must consider whether he persuades us that there is no issue of truth, no question of correctness, with respect to our beliefs about the world. Davidson so clearly opposes this view because he not only thinks there is more to be said about truth at a theoretical level, he also thinks that some of what has to be said is about our beliefs in an objective world.

In what follows I will discuss Davidson in some detail, while touching on Gadamer and Cavell. The central issue is whether Rorty's pragmatic clarifications and dismissals prevail over Davidson's promise of a philosophical theory of truth that is neither a correspondist nor a pragmatist one, but one that would enable us to judge some of our beliefs as true in a systematic way that transcends intralinguistic practice.

There is a great deal in Davidson's work that Rorty espouses and admires, particularly Davidson's holistic views on language and truth. But he balks at the implications for those views of Davidson's insistence that realism is a coherent and affirmable position. Rorty's misgivings do not arise from a commitment to nonrealism, but rather from a conviction he shares with Dewey, namely, that skepticism and the realist/nonrealist debate become hopeless philosophical muddles once correspondism is abandoned and the distinctions it generates and supports collapse. Davidson therefore poses a dilemma for Rorty. On the one hand Davidson is saying some sensible things about truth; on the other hand, he is doing *philosophy*. This means that Davidson offers his views on truth as contributions to philosophical theorizing, rather than as pragmatic dismissals of the issue, and takes seriously the implications of those views for realism. Davidson still practices what Rorty thinks should be abandoned. Rorty does not think philosophy can make a difference in the way that Davidson wants it to.[1] Davidson believes that his work constitutes progress with respect to truth; Rorty thinks the sort of philosophy Davidson wants to do is over, that it "culminated" in the work of Quine, Sellars, and the Davidson of "On the Very Idea of a Conceptual Scheme."[2]

Rorty tries to resolve the dilemma by reading Davidson as a pragmatist—albeit an unwitting one—and thereby placing him on a knife-edge between the end of the philosophical tradition and the beginning of latter-day Deweyan pragmatism. The main obstacle to Rorty's resolution is that, his conception of philosophy aside, Davidson ties his views on truth to the realist/nonrealist debate and puts himself squarely on the side of the realist. Davidson recognizes his views on truth could be misconstrued as having nonrealist implications. But Rorty does not believe the issue between realists and nonrealists is a coherent one, once the presuppositions of that debate are made clear. He sees Davidson, then, as sufficiently gripped by the mirror imagery of traditional philosophy to misconstrue pragmatism and the implications of his own position. Rorty tries to dispel Davidson's misconceptions by better characterizing pragmatism and drawing out what he considers the implications of Davidson's holism.

My primary concern in this chapter is not with Davidson's views but with Rorty's. However, a cautionary note is called for here about Davidson's views. I agree with Hacking that Davidson is not happy with being read as a pragmatist. But I have read and commented on Davidson's "A Nice Derangement of Epitaphs," and further agree with Hacking that Davidson may be in transition with respect to his views on language, and possibly also his views on truth.[3] It is possible, then, that Davidson might be moving somewhat closer to Rorty's interpretation. Nonetheless, Davidson takes the philosophical enterprise very seriously and would reject a purely historicist understanding of that enterprise and of his own contributions to it. The benefits of reading Davidson as a pragmatist, then, seem to have less to do with Davidson than with Rorty's peace of mind. Still, the question of whether Davidson's present views on truth can be read as pragmatic is an important one, having to do with whether or not philosophizing—at least about truth—can survive rejection of (Platonic) correspondism without becoming pragmatic. And at this time, Davidson's views constitute a position that is neither correspondist nor pragmatic, and that remains independent of further change in Davidson's own philosophical development.

NOT A THEORY OF TRUTH

Rorty thinks the rejection of scheme/content dualism has been Davidson's major contribution thus far.[4] He regards Davidson's arguments against scheme/content dualism, like Sellars's against "the given" and Quine's against analyticity, as nails in the coffin of mirror-imagery philosophy.[5] Without the possibility of "alternative conceptual schemes," a "given" to serve as "internal" cognitive foundations, or sameness of meaning as a test for *a priori* truth, traditional epistemology is not only impossible, but is revealed as a self-vitiating attempt to resolve spurious problems generated by premises designed to preclude such resolution. Moreover, along with the scheme/content distinction goes the possibility of "correspondence" between the world—as presented in our intuitions—and accurate (or inaccurate) conceptual structuring of those intuitions. So the only things we need say about truth, as we shall see below, have to do with the causality of belief. Because Davidson rejects (traditional) correspondism, Rorty takes Davidson's views on truth not as more theory but as a contribution to postphilosophical conversation. However, as Rorty himself points out in "Pragmatism, Davidson and Truth," Davidson has explicitly denied that he is a pragmatist.[6]

Rorty claims Davidson denies pragmatism because

> Davidson thinks of pragmatism as an identification of truth with assertibility, or with assertibility under ideal conditions. If such an identification is essential to pragmatism, then indeed Davidson is as anti-pragmatist as he is anti-empiricist. For such an identification would merely be an emphasis on the "scheme" side of an unacceptable

dualism, replacing the emphasis on the "content" side represented by traditional empiricism. Davidson does not want to see truth identified with anything.[7]

In short, Davidson construes pragmatism as a coherence theory and as implying idealism, as do Meynell and so many others. But Rorty does not think pragmatism, properly conceived, incorporates an identification of truth with anything at all. Davidson is said to accept the traditional, but distorted, conception of pragmatism as a philosophical alternative to correspondism that *analyzes* truth as "what works," or something similar. Rorty thinks that if Davidson can be made to construe pragmatism properly, he will understand the pragmatic nature of his own work.

Hilary Putnam has objected perhaps most clearly to the idea that pragmatism offers analyses of truth. Rorty refers to Putnam's argument, the gist of which is that attempting analyses of truth in terms of what works, or warranted assertibility, is comparable to trying to define "good" naturalistically. With regard to definitions of "good," it can always be asked of whatever goes on the right-hand side of the equation whether it is good. In a similar way, questions about truth and falsity are always applicable to whatever goes on the right-hand side of any "truth is . . ." equation. Putnam is right that if relating truth to warranted assertibility or something of the kind is deemed an analysis of "true," the relating must fail. Rorty readily admits that

> As Putnam notes . . . arguments against . . . *analyses* of "true" are as easy as Moore's arguments against attempts to define "good," and for pretty much the same reason. "True but not warranted assertible" makes as good sense as ". . . good but not conducive to the greatest happiness" or "good but disapproved of by all cultures . . . ."[8]

Against Putnam's and Davidson's presuppositions, Rorty argues that pragmatists offer formulas such as "warranted assertibility" either to relativize "the notion of truth to a language theory" or to show that "we do not need a notion of 'true' once we have the notion of 'warranted assertible.'"[9] So they are not offering analyses of truth. Incidentally, on this standard only Dewey gets top marks, for Peirce thought that his was at least something like an analysis of "true," and James often sounds as if he thought the same about his own account.

Pragmatism, then, offers not a competing theory of truth but a dismissal of such theories, a change of subject—at the risk of collapsing into some sort of idealist coherentism. However, some criticize as disingenuous the claim that pragmatism can be a change of subject regarding truth, as against a competing theory. James Young, for example, recently argued that my account of Rorty's avoidance of truth theories is disingenuous and that "Philosophers without a theory of truth are shirking their responsibilities."[10] The claim that one *can* change the subject with respect to truth, that truth is "what works" or that it is a redundant notion, meets resistance. The reason is that, whether as an analysis or not, pragmatism makes truth an intralinguistic feature in the sense that to describe a sentence as true is only to relate it to other sentences. This prompts the objection by realists, such as Putnam himself, that to make truth intra-linguistic *is* to adopt coherentism. Rorty acknowledges the danger, but thinks it only apparent, contending that Putnam's argument is based on the realist *presupposition* that only a position that relates sentences to the world will be satisfactory with respect to truth. Any other position, such as Dewey's understanding of truth as warranted assertibility that relates sentences to other sentences, will be seen as idealist or nonrealist. Putnam's argument intends not only to clarify how pragmatism cannot be an analysis of truth, but to thereby demonstrate that pragmatism is untenable. Contrary to this, Rorty tries to show that pragmatism, while not an analysis of truth, is still viable—as a turn away from hopeless theorizing.

Perhaps we can say this much: admittedly the pragmatist errs if she offers an analysis of "true" in terms of warranted assertibility or something similar, thereby opting for traditional coherentism and all its problems; and admittedly it is difficult to offer only an "account" of truth without sliding into analysis, as Peirce does. So Davidson's belief that pragmatists equate "true" with something like "warranted assertible" is not obviously wrong, and pragmatism, like correspondism, may violate his views on truth. The result is that to characterize Davidson as a crypto-pragmatist, Rorty must first make out his *general* claim that pragmatism is a changing of the subject with respect to truth, and not provision of an alternative—and inevitably coherentist—analysis of truth. Once the possibility of the change of subject is established, the spectre of skepticism will cease to haunt pragmatism. So in this particular case, Davidson must be made to reconstrue pragmatism, in order that he dismiss his concern with skepticism. Rorty does not see these as distinct tasks, though, for he thinks that a proper understanding that pragmatism does not offer an analysis of truth leads to abandonment of realism (or nonrealism) as a tenable position.

The characterization of Davidson's views in *Mirror* reflects the importance Rorty attaches to Davidson's work. (I can offer "hearsay" support of Rorty's assessment of Davidson's "On the Very Idea of a Conceptual Scheme," because Davidson, in conversation, put special emphasis on Rorty's interest in that paper, suggesting that much of Rorty's subsequent work involved development of the ideas it contains.)[11] Davidson's contribution in rejecting scheme/content dualism was part of what Rorty sees as the culmination of analytic philosophy. And while its historical importance is not diminished by Davidson's avowal of realism—it has influenced the intellectual move past analytic philosophy—Davidson's work on truth must be detached from the residual mirror imagery Rorty finds in the avowal of realism. However, before we consider Rorty's efforts to pragmatize Davidson's views on truth, more must be said about Davidson's rejection of the scheme/content distinction, or conceptual-scheme pluralism, and how it is seen by Rorty as grounds for Davidson's alleged pragmatism. We can then consider whether Rorty succeeds in collapsing Davidson's theorizing about truth into pragmatic clarification and so manages to expose worries about realism and skepticism as misconceived.

CONCEPTUAL SCHEMES AND HOLISM

Davidson's rejection of conceptual schemes, his views on truth, and his commitment to realism are, of course, interrelated. Davidson denies a split between experience and its organization, and denies that individual sentences are true in "corresponding" to delineable "facts." This much, at least, is compatible with pragmatism. But he also affirms realism. To understand Rorty's interest in Davidson one must appreciate how promising Davidson's denials look to a pragmatist and how disappointing is his affirmation of realism. With respect to the denial of the scheme/content distinction, Davidson's rejection of conceptual schemes as hopelessly elusive is paradigmatic of what Rorty considers productive in the resolution of traditional philosophical problems. Davidson showed the consequences of incorporating an untenable notion into our thinking; he showed us that something we think we discern, but in fact introduce, simply does not work as it is intended to work.

His holistic view of language underlies Davidson's rejection of conceptual-scheme pluralism as a philosophically viable explanatory notion. For Davidson, individual words have meanings only in terms of their roles in the whole of a language. This contrasts with the traditional view that links language to the world, by maintaining that at least some words have basic ostensive meanings and that other words "piggy-back" on them in constituting a language. Without the notion of basic ostensions "anchoring" language, the idea that those basic ostensions might vary among individual language-users or linguistic groups—and hence support alternative categorical structures or conceptual schemes—is untenable. In the holistic view, language ceases to be a system in which some elements are made meaningful and true by tight referential links to ideas and the world. Therefore, true sentences are not true in virtue of piecemeal accurate portrayal; nor are they made true by relatedness or "correspondence" to something they somehow picture. Sentences are not ideational or linguistic *simulacra* of states of affairs; nor are they meaningful as portraits or overt *simulacra* of "meanings" or ideas. A holistic view says the point of a theory of meaning is to give an account of how, in Davidson's words, "the meanings of sentences depend upon the meanings of words."[12] That is, there is no deep question about how words mean, no concern about relating them to "meanings" or "ideas." What we must understand is how "they have a systematic effect on the meanings of the sentences in which they occur."[13] Similarly, a theory of truth tries to say how sentences work in a language, not how certain juxtapositions of words replicate juxtapositions of things and events in some *non*empirical way.

Rorty sums up Davidson's holism by saying that "Davidson's neo-Wittgensteinian point is that even 'red' and 'mama' have uses . . . only in the context of sentences and thus of a whole language."[14] This view disallows "components" in thought and language, which can vary independently of one another and therefore call for theories that connect those components and guarantee invariance.

Rorty's interpretation of Davidson's holism is that the scheme/content distinction fails because it disjoins the notion of truth from that of meaning. The distinction attempts to carry the Kantian differentiation between concepts and intuitions into the philosophy of language as the idea that "every statement contain[s] our contribution (in the form of the meanings of component terms) as well as the world's (in the form of the facts of sense-perception)."[15] On the rejected reading, the "shape" of our contribution, the structure of our meanings, could differ from that of other individuals or groups. Therefore, the organization of "intuitions," or the world's contribution, could differ. Of course Kant himself would find this idea untenable, for his organizational categories were supposedly common and essential to being rational. But once the distinction is drawn between concepts and intuitions, and then between meanings and what meanings structure, there is no conclusive way to preclude systematic variance among sets of concepts and meanings. The result is that we are left with the possibility of alternative organizational concept-schemes. And in the area of language, we are left with meaning-structures that underlie languages and may differ enough from one another to preclude translations of the languages they support. The disjoining of truth from meaning makes possible variety of meaning that is independent of truth as evident in language-use.

Rorty considers that Davidson's most effective way of rejecting the scheme/content distinction was to point out that the notion of an "alternative conceptual scheme" is actually "the notion of a language which is 'true but not translatable.'"[16] Rorty then restates the heart of the argument by pointing out the

> connection between Davidson's holism about meaning and his disdain for the notion of "scheme". Someone who is not a holist . . . will think that understanding a language is a matter of two distinct processes—tying some individual words on the world via ostension, and then letting other words build up meanings around this central core . . . . He will also think that understanding what "truth" means involves "analyzing" every true sentence until ostensions which would make it true become apparent. This picture of holism ceasing to apply at the point at which reference is least problematic . . . is one way to get the scheme/content distinction going. . . . [W]e will be struck by the thought that somebody else will have "cut up" the world differently in their original acts of ostension.[17]

Davidson responds to the proposal that there might be diverse ways of organizing experience by maintaining that "if a difference in the original ostension does not show up at the holistic level—in the use of the sentences that contain the word—then the theory of meaning for the language can divide through by that difference."[18] The alleged difference, assuming it existed, would be wholly ignorable. There can be no point in puzzling about the matter. All we need do is understand how the language works, how individual terms play their roles in sentences, and how sentences are used.

Rorty's characterization of Davidson's argument is more succinct in *Consequences*:

> ... criticism of givenness [Sellars] and of analyticity [Quine] both serve to dismantle the Kantian notion of "conceptual frameworks" .... [W]ithout ... "the given" and ... "the a priori" there can be no notion of "the constitution of experience". [Davidson's] ... argument is verificationist, and turns on the unrecognizability of persons using a conceptual framework different from our own (or to put it another way, the unrecognizability as a *language* of anything that is not translatable into English).[19]

Once the underlying Kantian distinctions are abandoned as unviable mirror imagery, the notion that experience is diversely organized and results in varying meaning-structures becomes unintelligible. And that leads to the impossibility of describing something as a language that is in principle untranslatable because of unique basic ostensions.

Davidson's argument connects to Quine's rejection of "meaning" in this way: if speaking a language were a matter of expressing "meanings," those meanings might be structured in ways not exhaustively evident in what is said, as well as not related to the world as one's own language is. But as a consequence of this view, if one thinks of the activity of strangers who appear to be using a language backed up by "meanings" that must be discovered, thus construing understanding what the speakers *do* with their language as insufficient for understanding that language, one will be unable to differentiate between the strangers' using an alien "scheme" and their being wrong about a number of things. Consider an example used by Peter Hacker in conversation on this point: I may say "I wish Sunday came every Wednesday!" What I mean is something like "I wish I had more time."[20] If an alien translated my expression literally, it might conclude that my conceptual scheme tolerated contradictions, if the alien also understood how "Sunday" and "Wednesday" work in English. What is called for is clarification of the things we do with standard English for the sake of emphasis, dramatic impact, and so on. The apparent contradiction should tell the alien not that I have a different conceptual scheme, but that translations of English into alienese are still inadequate.

The alien is likely to ascribe an exotic conceptual scheme to someone saying "I wish Sunday came every Wednesday!" because doing so is preferable to believing that the speaker in question is systematically confused or wrong. In other words, when inadequate familiarity with a foreign language leads to oddities, and if the notion that meanings may vary independently of truth is accepted, it is clearly preferable to attribute oddities to divergent meaning-structures than to simple error or confusion. But then, if we accept that different ways of "cutting up the world" can explain difficulty in translation, we have to be prepared to attribute untranslatable languages "to *anything* that emits a variety of signals. But . . . this degree of open-endedness shows . . . that the purported notion of an untranslatable language is as fanciful as that of an invisible color."[21] Moreover, not only would the notion of an untranslatable language force indiscriminate ascription of language, it would mean we could not conclude, either in translation or mundane nontranslation cases, that someone using a language *was* wrong or confused, for it would always be possible to postulate a "scheme" or untranslatable language to "make sense" of nonsense.

Rorty does consider the likeliest objection, namely that Davidson can do no more than query verification of the existence of alternative languages or schemes. The core of Rorty's response is a distinction between ordinary and philosophically loaded senses of terms.[22] His point is to show that certain persistent philosophical questions about these terms rely on theory-laden versions of them, and he wants to jettison theory of this philosophical sort.

But this is where Rorty and Davidson part company. Davidson has provided a very powerful argument, and Rorty considers it the first major step toward recognizing the artifice of philosophical theorizing based on Kantian thinking. He thinks, then, that defense and development of the position require only clarification and demonstration of the hopelessness of certain substantive and methodological assumptions. But Davidson recognizes his holistic view will inevitably be seen as relativist or coherentist. Rorty blames those putative misconstruals on assessments of Davidson's holism that incorporate the very theses he rejects, and thinks what are called for are articulation of the presuppositions operant in that assessment and rejection of the enabling conditions for issues about realism and relativism. However, from Davidson's point of view arguments are needed against such misconstruals, and that means he admits and engages in philosophical theorizing. Davidson would consider himself successful if he showed his position to be a realist one in spite of his "soft" coherentism; Rorty is only prepared to accept withdrawal of the questions as misconceived.

Rorty contends that

> To suggest that Davidson is . . . [a] relativist in saying that most of our beliefs are true or that any language can be translated in English is just to say that he is not using the "Platonic" notions of Truth . . . and Reality which "realists" need to make their realism dramatic and controversial.[23]

But while I think Rorty is correct, we are still unconvinced that Davidson is a pragmatist. This is because Davidson *understands* reactions to his views that characterize them as relativistic or coherentist in some disturbing way. Rorty can understand those reactions only in the sense of understanding their historical antecedents and operant presuppositions. Davidson sees those reactions as defeasible in something like their own terms; Rorty considers them eliminable only through rejection of their enabling conditions. Rorty identifies Davidson's holism as common to his own position. And Rorty defends that holism against charges of coherentism and idealism on the grounds that the enabling conditions for those accusations are at issue and should be rejected. But Davidson does not follow suit. He appreciates the philosophical objections and the apparent implications of his holism and "correspondence from coherence" understanding of truth, and his response is to argue the realistic nature of his views. Rorty must judge that move as misconceived—as an inadvertent repudiation of Davidson's own rejection of the scheme/content distinction or conceptual-scheme pluralism—for the move grants that the enabling conditions of skepticism are still in place. And that is to allow that language and belief are still somehow related to, and anchored in, the world. Rorty must, then, attempt to deconstruct Davidson's affirmation of realism and thereby prevent Davidson's views on language and truth from being contaminated by mirror-imagery thinking. This not only preserves the force of the rejection of conceptual-scheme pluralism but also illuminates the pragmatic implications of that rejection. I shall now consider Rorty's effort to pragmatize Davidson's views on truth.

TRUTH

In "Pragmatism, Davidson and Truth" Rorty focuses on two topics: the pragmatic stance on truth and Davidson's construal of it, and Davidson's express commitment to realism. With respect to the truth issue, Rorty aims to show, through clarification of pragmatism, that Davidson misconstrues the pragmatic position regarding truth and that his rejection of correspondence is simply the pragmatic change of subject with respect to truth. Rorty's project here is no different from his general one of demonstrating that pragmatism abandons allegedly unproductive theorizing about truth.

Rorty sets out to clarify the pragmatic stance on truth by distinguishing between *critical* and *positive* remarks on truth; that is, between clarificatory comments and putative theoretical contributions. There is nothing importantly new in "Pragmatism, Davidson, and Truth" with respect to Rorty's position, but the discussion is perhaps clearer and more focused than in *Mirror* and *Consequences*. Rorty describes the critical pragmatic position on truth as one directed at "dissolution" of the traditional issues about truth. According to Rorty, the pragmatic claim is that "true" has no *explanatory* force, only a number of mundane uses. Specifically, these are a pair of normative uses and a "disquotational" use. The normative uses are those where "true" is interchangeable with "justified," and where "true" is contrasted with justification, as might be the case in explanations when we have good reason to believe something that is actually false. The disquotational use concerns remarks about remarks: in other words, descriptions of the conditions under which an utterance is said to be true. It is crucial for the pragmatist to explain the disquotational use. As the use which seems to be a comparison of statements with the world, it is the one most suggestive of correspondence.

Rorty claims that James neglected the second normative use as well as the disquotational use, but he sees in Davidson's views a way of giving "a place to all [these] uses while still eschewing the idea that the expediency of a belief can be explained by its truth"—that is, that beliefs are portraits of the world, and that sentences are linguistic renditions of those portraits and can themselves be judged accurate or inaccurate to the world, through their rendering of beliefs.[24] Because Davidson does not want to identify truth with accuracy—or anything else—his position on truth is regarded as consistent with the pragmatist's.

Rorty gives us, in "Pragmatism, Davidson and Truth," a very clear statement of the pragmatic position on truth. He articulates four propositions which allegedly clarify the sense in which "Davidson and James are both pragmatists":

(1) "True" has no explanatory use[;] (2) We understand all there is to know about the relation of beliefs to the world when we understand their causal relations with the world . . . . (3) There are no relations of "being made true" which hold between beliefs and the world[;] (4) There is no point to debates between realism and anti-realism, for such debates presuppose the empty and misleading idea of beliefs "being made true."[25]

In his discussion of Davidson, Rorty focuses on propositions two and four. Proposition two receives the most attention because Rorty does not really think proposition four is contentious. He thinks it follows from Davidson's espousal of the first and third, as well as from Davidson's general position. And here we see how Rorty's efforts to pragmatize Davidson's views on truth turn on eliciting Davidson's acceptance of the vacuity of skeptical doubts and hence of the pointlessness of asserting and defending realism. Davidson must be shown to accept proposition two.

Rorty and Davidson do agree on propositions one and three. There is nothing over and above the systematic convergence of belief and expressions of belief with how the world is. There is no *tertium quid*, no property or relation of correspondence that makes beliefs true by being common exclusively to true beliefs. (And in particular, it must not be thought that in virtue of some *tertium quid*, belief, like meaning in conceptual-scheme pluralism, might be structured in varying but nonevident ways and still adequately "fit" its causes.) Rorty wants to press the deconstructive point that if correspondence of belief to its objects is mistakenly conceived as something that varies independently of causal relations, then correspondence cannot be an explanatory notion, which is what those who so conceive it intend it to be.

Rorty thinks that proposition two yields proposition one; that we can go from asserting that understanding causal relations between beliefs and the world suffices for understanding knowledge and the use of (descriptive) language, to saying that truth is not an explanatory notion. However, the difficulty is to go from propositions one and three to two. That is, given Davidson's view that truth has no explanatory role because it does not make beliefs or sentences true, Rorty wants to claim that Davidson must accept that all there is to say about how beliefs relate to the world is to tell causal stories. To accept that is to preclude that anything of a philosophical nature can be said about the epistemic reliability of those causal stories. Given holism, all that is needed is *empirical* inquiry into the causal connections between belief and the world, so belief needs no philosophical justification that might bring its objects more reliably into line with its causes. But for the traditionalist, the causal stories yield no more than beliefs about causes, and hence do not get beyond coherence. And Davidson seems to agree. Rorty, however, insists that the very *intelligibility* of "getting beyond coherence"—that is, through correspondence—is what is at issue, and is being presupposed by the traditionalist who still considers epistemology a viable methodology for saying how the mind is the mirror of nature.

Much of the force of Rorty's argument in "Pragmatism, Davidson and Truth" is captured in the closing remark of the second section, where he describes Davidson's views on truth and the adequacy of "field" linguistics:

> On my interpretation, [Davidson's] argument that "coherence yields correspondence" comes down to "From the field linguist's point of view, none of the notions which might suggest that there was more to truth than the meaning of words and the way the world is are needed. So if you are willing to assume this point of view you will have no more skeptical doubts about the intrinsic veridicality of belief."[26]

The field linguist, engaged in practical translation, traces the hermeneutical circle until satisfied with practical results. She need not think that the natives are employing a different conceptual scheme, nor worry that beliefs might be systematically efficacious but still false or problematic. Nor should she consider herself engaged in discerning "meanings" behind what the natives say. What she has to do is interact and listen, test and retest. Rorty is convinced there is no intelligible way that belief, holistically construed, and language as a whole, can fail us. There are no awesome epistemological gaps to cross, so it makes no sense to declare ourselves realists. It would make sense only if language and belief mediated our commerce with an epistemologically distant world. But language and belief are part of the world. And it is here that Rorty approaches Gadamer's construal of truth. But, to proceed, we might ask this question: Why must Davidson be made a pragmatist if he could be a realist ally?

As indicated in the foregoing discussion, Rorty is unable to accept a realist ally because he thinks that the emptiness of debates about realism and skepticism follows the rejection of the idea that some *tertium quid* makes sentences and beliefs true. With truth neither discernible through transcendental arguments nor directly knowable in experience or *a priori*, there is no conceptual room for the idea that all intralinguistic justificatory criteria could be satisfied while allowing the possibility of systematic error, for sheer lack of contrast. There should be no Cartesian uncertainty, hence neither need nor room for realistic affirmations. Rorty thinks realist avowals are dangerous because they tolerate nonrealism as the contrasting notion that makes realism intelligible. To invoke realism is to invite the invocation of its opposite. Against this, Davidson is concerned that if realism is not invoked, the philosophical inclination will be to construe his views on truth and belief as nonrealist in nature. I think that Davidson is right, because our philosophical history has a certain momentum. It is not as if we were trying to prevent certain ideas or terms from becoming current. They are current. Here again there is an odd antihistoricist note in Rorty's line of argument. Davidson is acknowledging a history that Rorty—at least in this instance—apparently wants to forget. The fact is, even if we had abandoned mirror imagery when *Mirror* was published, we would still have the legacy of some 2500 years of it to contend with.

Rorty describes as his "chief textual evidence" for thinking Davidson holds proposition two—that inquiry into causal connection suffices with respect to understanding the relation of belief to the world—a passage about global skepticism that is in fact supportive of proposition two. Davidson says that

> What stands in the way of global skepticism of the senses is, in my view, the fact that we must, in the plainest and methodologically most basic cases, take the objects of a belief to be the causes of that belief. And what we, as interpreters, must take them to be is what they in fact are. Communication begins where causes converge: your utterance means what mine does if belief in its truth is systematically caused by the same events and objects.[27]

Rorty concurs with Davidson's view, but of course goes further, saying that " . . . there is nothing more to be known about the relation between beliefs and the rest of reality than what we learn from an empirical study of causal transactions between organisms and their environment."[28]

But Davidson's reliance on the sufficiency of causality is not a *de facto* dismissal of skeptical worries, as was D. M. Armstrong's claim about the "empirical sufficiency" of the majority of beliefs for objects being as believed to be.[29] Davidson is still interested in *defeating* skepticism by saying some beliefs are true—though not *made* true by correspondence. He contends that " . . . even a mild coherence theory like mine must provide a skeptic with a reason for supposing coherent beliefs are true."[30] In other words, there must be at least some philosophical or theoretical justification. Davidson thinks it insufficient to holistically relate belief to the world. He accepts that some philosophers will legitimately feel that doing so yields only a coherentist position that must eschew the idea that beliefs are *true*. Against Rorty's idea that Davidson's realism jeopardizes the rejection of the scheme/content distinction, Davidson fears that resting content with a coherentist position invites what he has rejected, namely, the scheme/content distinction. The reason is the same for Rorty and Davidson, namely, that it could be argued, given coherentism, that sets of beliefs might be variously structured and still relate adequately to their (postulated) causes. But whereas Rorty thinks a coherentist understanding of pragmatism or of Davidson's views can be blocked, Davidson thinks such a construal of his views must be answered. Rorty's textual evidence, then, is not conclusive. Additionally, there is a passage that poses a particular problem for Rorty, where Davidson remarks that he wants to say how, even if we

> cannot get outside our beliefs and our language so as to find some test other than coherence, we nevertheless can have knowledge and talk about an objective public world which is not of our making.[31]

This passage is difficult for Rorty, since it draws precisely the distinction between belief and the world that he claims pragmatism obviates. Rorty must question why there is any need to speak of a *test*. Any such test will be *epistemic* in nature; and Rorty allows only causal accounts of the relation of belief to the world. That is, his pragmatism cannot tolerate the meaningfulness of an inability to "find some test other than coherence." Why should coherence be thought of as a test, and an inadequate one at that? It is immediately suggested that we are worse off than we might be if, for instance, we had recourse to correspondence. Davidson not only tolerates the skeptical question; in trying to answer it he conceives of coherence as open to testing and so calling for philosophizing. Rorty repudiates the idea that the notion of such testing is (ultimately) intelligible. If the notion seems to make sense, it is only because we are still concerned to establish belief or "the mind" as a reliable mirror of nature or the world.

Davidson requires that we say how we have knowledge and refer to an objective world, in spite of being confined to our beliefs and language.[32] In this he is at odds with Rorty and Gadamer, neither of whom is willing to juxtapose knowledge or belief to an object-world. According to Rorty, we should not think in terms of being "confined" to beliefs and language; to do so is to allow questions about how we might—*per impossible*—get out of language and beliefs. Nor is this a one-sided debate. Davidson specifically notes that Rorty thinks this a confused issue.[33]

In brief, then, Rorty thinks that Davidson's espousal of the first and third of the propositions listed above, namely, that "true" has no explanatory role and that nothing makes beliefs true, commits Davidson to the second: that we understand all there is to understand about the relation of belief to the world when we understand the operant causal relations. Rorty then maintains that the fourth proposition—that there is no point to the realist/nonrealist debate—follows from the second. He thinks that without the idea of beliefs being made true by correspondence, the issue between realists and their opponents cannot arise.

I want to make a proposal about Rorty's reading of Davidson. The proposal is tentative because it turns on charging Rorty with either a bit of sleight of hand or a small *petitio*. To return to Rorty's four propositions, Davidson subscribes to the first and third, that "true" has no explanatory role and that nothing makes beliefs true; and he rejects the notion that anything makes beliefs true in the sense of being a property common only to beliefs that accurately portray their causes. But Rorty reads that as implying that the notion of beliefs *being* true is or should be rejected by Davidson, in the sense that there is no room to describe beliefs—or sentences—as true beyond the mundane ways we confirm or endorse what people say and believe. Rorty wants to preclude *philosophical* discourse about the truth of beliefs and sentences. And that is just what Davidson wants to preserve against the skeptic: our ability to say, in a *non*mundane way, that some beliefs are true. Rorty has taken Davidson's rejection of the idea that beliefs can be *made* true to imply that beliefs should not be described as *being* true in any but a mundane sense. This is, however, not to elicit Davidson's putative pragmatism; it is to presume that pragmatism, while disallowing Davidson's concern with how beliefs can be considered true in a theoretical sense.

Like Davidson, Rorty believes that all there is to the truth of what we say is how words are used and how things are. He also thinks, again like Davidson, that we cannot inquire into either meaning or facticity without inquiring into both. It is crucial that there is no third thing to be considered: no common property or "relation of correspondence." So when we decide that a statement or belief is true, saying so is not *explaining* anything; there is no room for theoretical or philosophical amplification. But Rorty, unlike Davidson, thinks that once we understand that we cannot establish beliefs or sentences as true extralinguistically, we should abandon any thought, much less any theorizing, about how our beliefs and language relate to the world—beyond the causal stories we tell *in* language. In short, Rorty sees no point in asking ahistorical questions or developing transcendental arguments. And he is in effect trying to prevent Davidson from doing transcendental philosophy.

For Rorty's efforts to read Davidson as a pragmatist to succeed, his clarifications and development of Davidson's views must compel a shift of perspective. We—and Davidson—should realize that avowals of realism are otiose, if not misconceived. There should be a response of "Aha!"; we should think "Of course, once . . . " But we seem to be left with two competing positions, and so with an issue. The notion persists that our beliefs are extralinguistically true; it has not become meaningless. In fact, we may wonder how Rorty manages to see it as meaningless, and what he draws on in dismissing the issue of realism. There is a deep question here about the adopting and discarding of philosophical perspectives. In the traditional view, change of this perspectival sort was supposedly produced by transcendental argument, with Kant's polemics against Humean empiricism the model. But Rorty rejects the methodology that makes such arguments possible. In the next section I want to consider what enables Rorty to proceed as he does. The answer is as much in the Continental thought Rorty admires as in his appropriations of Dewey and James.

THE CONTINENTAL CONNECTION

As indicated in chapter 1, I cannot hope to do justice here to Rorty's connection to thinkers like Gadamer and Derrida. However, the brief remarks I made about Gadamer in the previous chapter must be supplemented in order to provide a paradigm that will help us to better understand Rorty. It is important at this juncture to understand how Rorty can deal with Davidson as he does without at least begging questions or relativizing or trivializing philosophy. Hermeneutics constitutes a model of postphilosophical discourse, as we noted in the last chapter and as Rorty himself suggests in the third part of *Mirror*. The historicity of hermeneutics is a march on traditional philosophy, even if it falls short of Deweyan pragmatism, and the outrageous pseudopolemics of Derrida remind us that solemn Kantian apodictic philosophizing is, after all, only "a kind of writing."[34] But in order to appreciate Rorty's reliance on hermeneutics, we must begin with his inability to see how his own philosophical tradition can provide what he needs. I think this inability is perhaps clearest in Rorty's disagreement with Stanley Cavell.

Cavell, like Davidson, takes skepticism seriously, and he too is challenged on the point by Rorty. But there is no attempt to read Cavell as a pragmatist; instead, the objective is to show the wrongness of his position. What is significant about Rorty's view of Cavell, unlike his view of Davidson, is that it accuses Cavell of muddling two very different things, namely, a hopelessly academic skepticism and a "Kantian, Romantic" notion about the possibility that our language and beliefs might somehow fail to fit the world. Davidson at least tackled a serious matter—even if he retained the intelligibility of skepticism—in that his target was the very sophisticated notion of organizations of experience varying in ways not evident in language. Cavell is apparently trying to lend seriousness to much less sophisticated worries about perceptual veracity that have been with us since Cratylus. In doing so Cavell is considered guilty of trying to take us back to a pre-Kantian context. Whatever was wrong with Kant's distinction between concepts and intuitions, he took us beyond Cartesian ideas and Humean impressions by thinking that the foundations of knowledge were propositions and not objects. Rorty accuses Cavell of trying to undo the work of both Kant and Sellars by construing skepticism of the senses as he does.

Rorty concludes the section "Cavell on Skepticism," a reading of the first two parts of Cavell's *The Claim of Reason*, with the following remark:

My complaints about Cavell's treatment of skepticism may be summed up by saying that his book never makes this possibility [of relating "textbook" epistemology to the sense "of the contingency of everything"] clear for someone for whom it is not yet an actuality.[35]

Cavell tries to relate philosophical skepticism to something we might describe as the deep realization of contingency. He thinks that philosophical skeptical doubts are abstract summations of such realizations. Speaking of Price's favored example of an object of (questionable) perception, a tomato, Cavell says that "All of existence is squeezed into the philosopher's tomato when he rolls it toward his overwhelming question."[36] Rorty considers this a confusion. He says, "Kant's phenomenal world is not Price's tomato on a grand scale."[37]

Rorty cites as Cavell's basic error the view that a Continental philosopher struggling with *angst* is doing the same kind of thing as a British epistemologist puzzling about the reality of a tomato, and that the only differences between them are cultural and historical—notational, in effect. This characterization of Cavell's project is not unfair. For example, Cavell has linked the academic problem of other minds with *King Lear*.[38] He seems to think that puzzling about how we might know that the bodies we encounter have minds and experiences as we do, or hammering out arguments such as Bertrand Russell's Analogy argument, are only more markedly academic concerns than trying to understand how Lear's elder daughters can come to see and treat him as they do. Cavell tries to show that Anglo-American epistemology always *has* been concerned with the issues usually identified with Continental philosophy, hence with deeper matters and a broader spectrum of intellectual questions than is usually thought. And in this way Cavell attempts to narrow the gap between academic epistemology and the hermeneutical, or other Continental, traditions.

In pursuing the comparison of Anglo-American epistemology and Continental philosophy, Rorty contrasts standard attempts by philosophical analysts to "deromanticize" Continental philosophy with Cavell's efforts to "romanticize our own tradition."[39] There is good reason to disavow the former tendency for complacent "analytic" philosophers to argue that if there is anything of merit in, say, hermeneutics, it must be just "good philosophy" done in a different idiom. This view implies that one need not work at understanding thinkers like Gadamer or Derrida, since whatever they are saying that is of value will be available in one's own idiom. As I have argued elsewhere, this is at the very least a radical underestimation of differences in traditions.[40] Rorty understands this, and he will not countenance the philosophical reduction implied by the "deromanticization" of Continental philosophy.

But neither will Rorty approve of the philosophical enhancement of epistemology that is an objective of Cavell's enterprise. Edifying philosophy of the kind Rorty attributes to Wittgenstein, Heidegger, and Dewey cannot be accommodated by a view that enhances Price's—or Davidson's—brand of philosophy. If both Price and Gadamer are doing *philosophy*, as Cavell implies, there is no room for Deweyan or Wittgensteinian critiques or Heideggerian "new words." That is because the latter are supposed to be *new* conversations, while in Cavell's view the problems or issues—deep contingency, say—are separate from styles of philosophizing. Conversations may therefore vary independently of their topics, and their novelty will be stylistic or perspectival. Both Cavell and Davidson think there are perennial philosophical problems, so there are questions that are ahistorical in form if not in particular content.

What emerges from Rorty's treatment of Cavell is that an attempt to enhance academic epistemology, if successful, would preclude the novelty Rorty claims for edifying philosophy by making that novelty perspectival or stylistic rather than total in the sense of incorporating both new discourses and new subject matters. This is too serious an error in Rorty's view. Cavell's project cannot be salvaged because it is too dangerous, and in any case he offers nothing interesting—though Rorty thinks he does in the area of ethics. On the other hand, Davidson's concern with realism seems exorcisable and is tied to a hugely productive argument and a rejection of correspondism. Davidson poses both an impressive challenge and a potentially great victory: certainly enough for productive conversation.

I want to stress here that Rorty's intolerance of both Davidson's avowal of realism and Cavell's aggrandizement of Pricean epistemology is consistent with his conception of philosophical activity as either humdrum or edifying. Philosophy may be edifying when a Dewey or a Wittgenstein overturns our intellectual assumptions in a Kuhnian "paradigm shift." But edifying philosophy must remain rare, as it is the production of a wholly new perspective, the initiation of a new conversation. Against this, humdrum philosophizing is a matter of continuing the conversation, exploring implications, clarifying positions, testing for consistency, unearthing presuppositions, and so on. The trouble with seriously considering skepticism and the realist/nonrealist debate is that it is neither edifying to do so nor productive in a humdrum way: it is in fact a pointless conversation. All that can be gained already has been, either in a "local" sense, by John Austin's rebuttals of A. J. Ayer, or in a grander manner, by Wittgenstein's and Dewey's dismissals of the issues. Speaking of Cavell's consideration of skepticism, Rorty notes that

Cavell's point that skepticism only makes sense for generic objects shows just what he doesn't want to show—that one can leave Ayer and Price in the care of Austin and Ryle, and hasten on to the serious thinkers.[41]

But who are the serious thinkers, and why is it so important to isolate their work from that of Price and others like him? The serious thinkers, at least the contemporary ones, are those who, like Gadamer, are enriching culture rather than pursuing academic philosophy. They have gone beyond mirror imagery and do not presume to raise ahistorical questions or make ahistoricist pronouncements. Rorty draws support from the projects of people like Gadamer and Derrida, for he believes they illustrate the variety of intellectual pursuits that can coexist in, and enrich, our culture, without pretensions of methodological correctness or ahistorical implications. That intellectual variety, which affords viable alternatives to Davidsonian analytic thinking, together with the currency of those alternatives, provides proof that no single philosophy can be the one and only *right* sort which must underlie—and legitimize—any intellectual project. Projects like Gadamer's, because they are hermeneutical, are self-consciously historicist in avoiding just the methodological claims to unique or privileged status implicit in Davidson's attempt to defeat skepticism while at least qualifying correspondism. So those projects provide a perspective from which Rorty can be critical of Davidson's enterprise, without quitting the intellectual game even as he abandons what many consider necessary methodological criteria and procedures. Specifically, he can dismiss interest in the realism debate without ignoring a legitimate issue—or worse, appearing not to understand it.

The trouble is that Rorty's models—Gadamer's views on truth comprise the most pertinent example—seem more vulnerable to traditional philosophical methodological questions than Rorty might allow. Most significantly, they seem vulnerable to the issue of validation, as mentioned earlier, in spite of Rorty's efforts to show that raising such issues is only a manifestation of the retention of unworkable distinctions and techniques. Nor is the issue of validation forced on Gadamer; it arises from his own claims.

Gadamer conceives of truth neither as a relation of ideational or sentential items to facts, nor—as is evident in his focus on the interpretation of texts—as a relation of sentences to ideas. Against Emilio Betti and others, Gadamer repudiates the idea that interpretation of texts, or for that matter of remarks, is a question of discerning ideas through the understanding of sentences. He views truth as a special sort of *placement* of the understanding subject in a tradition. Gadamer puts great weight on what he calls "effective history" and on awareness of that history. In this way it seems a model of what Rorty endorses against Davidson's efforts to continue epistemology. Josef Bleicher tells us that

> The central argument of hermeneutic philosophy can best be illustrated by reference to the title of Gadamer's book, *Truth and Method*. Method has, since Descartes, represented the royal road to truth in the sense of *veritas* and *adaequatio intellectus ad rem*: the correspondence between fact and proposition. The truth of the latter could be ascertained by reference to the former. . . . Heidegger's monumental re-directing of philosophy rests on counterposing this propositional truth with another kind: *alethia* (disclosure).[42]

This "disclosure" is offered to us in place of the correspondence of belief and sentences to states-of-affairs, and of conclusions validated by transcendental arguments. Any secure methodology for arriving at ahistorical truth is abandoned. Nonetheless, Gadamer talks of truth, and "disclosure" is not mere consensus, so the ambiguity about validation persists. How *are* conclusions deemed true, either in consensus or in awareness of effective history and location of self in a tradition?

Gadamer, developing Heidegger's view, conceives of truth as a level of understanding, a "fusing of horizons," which incorporates consciousness of history and "prejudices"; it is a kind of situatedness in a historical context—a situatedness recognized through consensus and dialogue. To quote Bleicher quoting Gadamer,

> Gadamer states that "Understanding is not to be thought of so much as an action of one's subjectivity, but as the placing of oneself within a tradition, in which past and present are constantly fused" (pp. 274–5, 258 [*Truth and Method*]). It is this insight that obsessive concern with method has obscured.[43]

But Bleicher nonetheless asks the crucial question: "How are we able to separate legitimate from arbitrary prejudices?"[44] How do we judge that the "fusing of horizons" is proceeding properly? Rorty would answer that *productivity* is the sole criterion. But Gadamer makes the Heideggerian move of stressing the medium-nature of language against its representational or portrayal role. In other words, we need worry about truth only while we continue to conceive of language as something *between* us and the world, as something we use to portray how things are. Gadamer, following Heidegger's dictum that "language is the house of Being," reconstrues language as the medium in which understanding occurs; and understanding is a mode of being, rather than a qualification of mind facilitated by language.[45] There can be no question of the adequacy of language to anything whatever. It is simply our mode of understanding and being, in that it is our mode of being as understanding entities. Truth is no longer a matter of how language relates to anything else, but of how we are constituted at some point; how we *are* as subjects; how we are located in our traditions—that is, in language. Gadamer insists that

> The fundamental relation of language and world does not . . . mean that the world becomes the object of language. Rather, the object of knowledge and of statements is already enclosed within the world horizons of language. The linguistic nature of the human experience of the world does not include making the world into an object.[46]

Gadamer's view is very much like Rorty's, because for Rorty language cannot be compared against the world—hence there is no question of truth in the sense of adequacy of propositional rendition. In *Mirror* he precisely labels the philosophy of language just another veil-of-ideas exercise, in the sense that language only replaces the sense-data of earlier epistemology as the "new" mediator between the world and the knowing mind.[47]

Gadamer stretches the limits of language to enclose all "Being"; nothing is left for us that is not language. Language encompasses both our being as understanding entities and what we understand. There is no "object" world. Being that is understandable or intelligible is language.[48] And for us, as conceptualizing, understanding beings, what is not understandable is wholly unthinkable; affirmation of its existence must be meaningless. It is as if Kant's phenomenal realm were identified with what there is, and the noumenal, precisely because it is beyond experience—in this case language—were simply jettisoned as meaningless. This is pretty much what Rorty wants in his pragmatism: an abandonment of the Kantian distinction. Neither Rorty nor Gadamer wants the Kantian distinction abandoned as an affirmation of only half of that distinction, of course, but whether it can be otherwise abandoned is precisely what is at issue.

The noumenal must be eradicated as an idea; no philosophical contrast should be tolerated if it allows room for skeptical doubts *within* the linguistic, which exhausts what there is though somehow not in an ontological sense. That is why Davidson's defense of realism is misconceived and must be exorcised. Philosophical *theory* can only attempt to get beyond the linguistic through transcendental arguments. But if there is *nothing* beyond language—and we cannot even say nothing intelligible— then efforts at such theorizing must be pointless, and truth cannot be any sort of faithful mirroring. The last thing truth can be is correspondence between ideas or sentences and states of affairs as extralinguistic. To the tradition all of this naturally looks like idealism; the Kantian distinction, or something like it, persists. But with respect to truth in particular, the trouble is that, as Bernstein puts it,

> many of the problems that Gadamer leaves unsolved are related to the ambiguities he allows concerning the meaning or truth, and specifically concerning the validation of the "claims to truth" that tradition makes upon us. And here one must frankly admit that there is a danger of lapsing into relativism. I have argued Gadamer is really committed to a communicative understanding of truth, believing that "claims to truth" always implicitly demand argumentation to warrant them, but he has failed to make this view fully explicit. He also fails to notice how this ambiguity transforms much of the rest of what he says. For although all claims to truth are fallible and open to criticism, they still require validation—validation that can be realized only through offering the best reasons and arguments that can be given in support of them.[49]

Even if we abandon (Platonic) correspondism and its notion of an objective, uninterpreted reality, we are left with the need to validate truth-claims. And surely that is all Davidson needs or wants. In a crucial passage in "On the Very Idea of a Conceptual Scheme" he tells us that

In giving up the dualism of scheme and world, we do not give up the world, but reestablish unmediated touch with the familiar objects whose antics make our sentences and opinions true or false.[50]

But this is precisely where Rorty and Davidson differ. Davidson agrees with Bernstein and proceeds to work very hard at providing validation, at giving reasons why our beliefs about the world are true even without a relation of correspondence between them and their subject-causes. Nor does Davidson offer transcendental arguments in the traditional sense; that is, he does not try to reach out beyond language and belief. Davidson's work is so special and contemporary because it avoids being putatively transcendental in this unworkable way. Very roughly, Davidson wants the world that determines the truth of our beliefs to be *accessible*; he is not introducing notions such as "the noumenal"; he wants to say how our beliefs are true within a realist understanding, in spite of the acknowledgment that the connection of language to the world, and the determination of belief by the world, can only be *philosophically* described and understood holistically. Rorty, like Gadamer, considers affirmations of realism hopeless attempts to put in place an "objective" world outside language—outside understanding—and thereby quell a Cartesian fear that what we know and do and say is somehow without grounds. And, perhaps worse, those affirmations manifest a belief in a secure and universally overriding methodology capable of yielding apodictic conclusions; or they at least prelude a search for such a methodology. And if Rorty is against anything, it is belief in, or felt-need of, a philosophical methodology. But what is important for my present purpose is that, though for somewhat different reasons, neither Gadamer nor Rorty sees his position as perverse indifference to an epistemological issue, or as a denial of truth or objectivity and a *de facto* opting for an idealist coherentism.

It should now be appreciated, as a fact that seems to straddle the line between philosophy and psychology, that if we retain Davidson's view that validation of our beliefs is called for in principle, then we will not have understood the pragmatic or hermeneutic "vision," and we will still see realism as an *issue*. If we fail to take Rorty's perspective, if we feel that it is *he*, not Davidson, who jeopardizes realism, we are left with the difficult question of deciding what weight to give to that fact—or to the corresponding perspective. This issue—the significance of the *currency* of a view or perspective—is at the heart of historicism. As I shall suggest in the next chapter, it cannot be decided on its own grounds; we cannot prove or disprove historicism. But we can consider carefully the question of whether there is real *progress* in intellectual inquiry. Rorty must abandon the notion of progress, and here he is at odds with Dewey. But his pragmatism is at bottom a denial that we can ever be in a position to consider something or some intellectual turn as *progress*, except insofar as it proves more productive than whatever went before. In other words, progress, like truth, must be judged intralinguistically and intraperspectivally. Again as we shall see in the next chapter, that is what makes the status of science so crucial a matter for Rorty. Science at least claims real progress independent of historical factors.

At the present juncture, we can respond in one of three ways to Rorty on the issue of truth: accept the viability of Davidson's enterprise in spite of Rorty's contentions—in effect, ignore him; attempt to demonstrate the effectiveness of transcendental arguments, which would surely be misconceived and play into Rorty's hands; or more modestly suggest that a continued acceptance of realism as coherent is neither self-delusion nor a failure to understand the Rortyan critique. Developing the latter position is my main concern in this book and is, I believe, a matter of providing a sympathetic exposition of Rorty—one which makes reasonable understanding of his position evident—and then putting the burden on him to show where we have not understood. Demonstrating that we are not self-deluded in taking Davidson seriously is a matter of using the pragmatist's own arguments, for if we understand the critique and can still hold our realist position, the onus of showing the failure of our perspective shifts to the pragmatist. In the next section I want to pull together some of the foregoing points, to show how the issue of realism persists, and hence how Davidson's views on truth resist pragmatic interpretation.

CONCLUSION

Rorty will not tolerate philosophical theorizing, for he thinks it presupposes, or at least aspires to, a methodology having transcendental power. Such a methodology underlies and serves to adjudicate all other intellectual enterprises, and can help us reach out beyond language and belief to an ultimate reality. In rejecting traditional philosophy, Rorty rejects above all the conception of philosophy as *the* method for arriving at ahistorical truth—a super science whose subject matter is rationality itself and ultimate reality.[51] Rorty asks us to realize the futility of attempting to develop philosophical methodology and trying to theorize ahistorically.

He directs us to transfer the weight of our concern with truth and other philosophical topics from the theoretical to the mundane level, by maintaining that there is no legitimate theoretical level for such concern. We are being asked to be more comfortable in the world; to *accept* that things are as they are and that we often know and say how they are, without looking for a theoretical explanation of how we are able to do so.

To borrow a term from another discipline, we are asked not to introduce the economic notion of *surety*—something that guards against default—into our talk about sentences and beliefs. More accurately, Rorty warns us not to misconstrue talk about truth *as* talk about surety. Davidson's antiskeptical polemics are paradoxical to Rorty, because if Davidson has eschewed surety with respect to individual true sentences, and if he insists on the sufficiency of causality and convergence, then he should not engage in antiskeptical polemics, since any stand on skepticism legitimates puzzlement about the availability of surety.

But Davidson seems to emerge the hero of the piece. The trouble, as noted above, is that we cannot easily rid ourselves of our philosophical heritage—unfortunate though it might be. Even Davidson's mild coherentism is still a relatively novel position that *contrasts with* the one in place, and therefore seems required to provide us with the possibility for certainty afforded by its correspondist rival. Rorty would disagree, arguing that what is in place is not a *theory* but a confusion, and that what counts in any case is whether a novel view is taken up. We cannot presuppose the standards of a view that is being rejected in assessing its proposed replacement. But this currency criterion works both ways. The continuation of Davidson's discourse cannot be dismissed. This is a point I want to stress. As I hope to have shown in the previous sections, Davidson's project retains its intelligibility and plausibility even when we understand what Rorty is up to. And it should not do so, if Rorty is correct.

But then Rorty cannot and does not want to be *right*. He must rely only on our taking up his view and losing interest in Davidson's. But when that does not happen, as I think it has not, he must be careful not to beg the question by saying we have *not* understood because of our realist presuppositions. Like Gadamer, he wants us to be able to adopt new perspectives by understanding our own "prejudices." But, also like Gadamer, he can neither force understanding with argument nor offer validation beyond productivity even when understanding occurs. We are left wondering, then, what to make of the currency of Davidson's enterprise. Is it to be dismissed as the momentum of academic philosophy and the unwillingness of its practitioners to enter a new conversation? Or does it constitute the legitimate continuation of epistemology? All Rorty can do to resolve this point is continue the conversation in the hope of either eliciting presuppositions in ways that make us abandon them or intriguing us enough to discard the Davidsonian perspective. That explains in part his profligacy and the somewhat repetitious tone of much of his writing. Rorty can only reiterate his pragmatic points in different styles and from different angles. The variety of styles and topics in *Consequences*, together with the tenacity of its pragmatic message, suffices to show this. And, with respect to the issue of truth, he explicitly remarks that he does not know how to *argue* against the traditional philosophical perspective: " . . . I have no arguments against . . . the claim that 'only the *world* determines truth.' "[52]

Davidson believes that it *is* the world that determines truth, even though it does not *make* beliefs or sentences true by virtue of some special property or relation such as "correspondence." So Davidson does not consider the issue of realism problematic in itself. Rorty is concerned that if we think the world determines truth, and if truth is not intralinguistic, then we immediately introduce a sense of truth that casts belief as the problematic reflection of an epistemologically distant reality—one that can be reached in cognition only through a methodology with transcendental power. Against this

> The pragmatist has no notion of truth which would enable him to make sense of the claim that if we achieved everything we ever hoped to achieve by making assertions we might still be making *false* assertions, failing to "correspond" to something.[53]

So Davidson's avowals of realism can only reintroduce the notion that our beliefs might not be true, in the sense that they could be systematically efficacious and yet be false by being somehow *different* from uninterpreted states of affairs: in other words, an effective but less than accurate conceptual scheme.

But this is not what Davidson is up to. As I read Davidson, he wants only to reassure the skeptic that our beliefs are *true*—not that they are efficacious because they "fit" reality in its uninterpreted state. Davidson's "mild coherence" view raises the question of whether our beliefs about the world, because not individually demonstrable as true through correspondence, might be false yet efficacious. But the possibility of that efficacy need not be explained in terms of conceptual schemes and uninterpreted reality; it can be interpreted in terms of approximations to truth, coincidental success, and so on. A parallel is the confirmation and falsification of theories in science. We can think of a theory as efficacious because it happens to work, even though no theory can accurately replicate or capture "ultimate reality," which is a scheme/content dualist idea; or we can judge as false a theory that happens to be working. For instance, a theory about infection which atttributes contamination to exchanges of animal spirits instead of germs would be wrong, but it might be efficacious for some time because it would support hygienic practices. We can doubt the truth of what we believe without having to distinguish between belief (as the mind's mirroring of nature) on the one hand and an uninterpreted reality (which is what is somehow mirrored) on the other. It is interesting that James's pragmatic arguments for the viability of religious faith failed precisely because of the sort of doubt that underlies Davidson's worries about realism. No one accepted James's suggestion that religious faith was *useful*; they insisted that it was *true*.

For Rorty, questions about "tests" for coherency are meaningless; for Davidson, questions about "tests" are questions regarding what we can best say about how we are limited to belief and language. To mention Armstrong again, he thought that the real issue of realism was whether we could *know* we know, and he concluded we could not, but that it made no important difference; we had to accept the "empirical" sufficiency of having certain beliefs.[54] Davidson is not, in my opinion, offering transcendental arguments to demonstrate we know what we know. Rather, he is allowing room for philosophical doubt and trying to answer that doubt by offering good reasons for thinking that we *do* know (most) of what we know. Rorty thinks talk like that is fruitless and dangerous, for it invites skepticism. He does not want us to acknowledge our epistemic limitations because to do so necessarily postulates something beyond them, as Gadamer thinks that to objectify a world beyond language is to fail to understand our linguistic nature. The pragmatist cannot think that a productive perspective might be false, whereas the nonpragmatist must construe productivity as a function of truth.

The burden of this chapter has been to show that, in spite of sympathetic clarification, Rorty's pragmatic views do not impose themselves on us. Because there is still an issue, that may seem a very minor victory or result, but reflection should show that it is in a way all we can expect and all we need. What we have is roughly this: Davidson offers a theory of truth that denies correspondence but leaves room for realism. In offering his theory Davidson acknowledges that while truth is not "correspondence to the facts," it is about how the world *is* and how it determines what we say and believe. He gets a kind of correspondence from holistically juxtaposing language and belief to the world—not a Kantian noumenal world, just the world. The world still determines truth, but without serving as a *relatum* in a correspondence relation that *makes* some sentences or beliefs true. A *theory* of truth is not about ideational and sentential piecemeal portrayal, but about truth-conditions: how a sentence works in a language, and hence when it is true. And—crucially—a large number of sentences work as they do when there is convergence of description and belief, when we say how things *are*. Unfortunately, it is just then that we are tempted to think that those sentences replicate situations. But as Hacking summarizes,

> There is no local correspondence, "the river" to the river. There is only total correspondence of all true sentences to the fact of everything; but this fact, the world, has no autonomy beyond what we say. That is [how] "coherence yields correspondence".[55]

When things are put this way, Rorty should not object to our conclusion that, even without "local" correspondence, which might assure us of the truth of our sentences and beliefs, our beliefs and sentences—holistically conceived—are true because of how the world is. But he objects to saying *anything at all* about the world as a determinant of truth. To do so invites questions about how we can be *sure*, and that is to persist in doing futile epistemology. In Gadamerian terms, Rorty does not want the world objectified as something over and against what we believe and say about it. Like Gadamer he wants us to acknowledge that we are totally immersed in language, and that "the world" is not something *separate*. And that is when it looks to many as if he has opted for a view that renders the epistemological status of the world problematic in trying to make that status redundant. Also like Gadamer, Rorty leaves us unconvinced.

The lack of conviction is actually a different conviction, namely, that it makes sense to wonder if our beliefs are true independently of intralinguistic considerations. We still think that the sorts of things we say in language about sentences and beliefs are dependent on how sentences and beliefs relate to the world beyond language. We may appreciate that that relatedness is not one of portrayal or of "local" correspondence, but we also appreciate that because one account of that relatedness—Platonic correspondism—is unviable, it does not follow that *no* account can be adequate because the very idea of that relatedness is somehow inherently confused. In short, we are unwilling to equate the dismantling of Platonic correspondism with the destruction of the very idea of truth as determined by the world. This point is clearest when we qualify correspondism as Platonic, and that is possible when someone like Davidson proposes an understanding of correspondence that is not Platonic. The nub of our discussion, then, is that the very intelligibility of Davidson's notion of holistic correspondence makes possible Davidson's realistic avowals.

Rorty's only option is to construe Davidson's holistic correspondence as a restatement of pragmatism. In so doing he is trying to disallow the Davidsonian conversation. That is, he and Davidson are partners in the rejection of Platonic correspondism, but they part company because each wants to replace the correspondist "conversation" with one of his own: Davidson with a recognizable philosophical one, Rorty with a rather novel postphilosophical one. In this way Rorty shows that while, to his credit, he does not see himself as an edifying philosopher on a par with his philosophical heroes, he cannot help being edifying to some extent—in his own sense of the term. That is, Rorty is edifying to the extent that he is a reactive thinker, that he writes with a view to exposing the pretensions of the tradition, that he deliberately provokes us in making his pragmatic points against correspondism, and that he wants to change our discourse. The significance of this is that edification in Rorty's sense is compound: it has a critical part—the rejection of an established tradition—and a positive part—the initiation of a new conversation. This means that there is a difference between Rorty's critical remarks on the (Platonic) correspondist tradition and his attempts to preclude Davidson's realist avowals. It is not a difference he is willing to tolerate, but it is one we can acknowledge once we recognize that Platonic correspondism does not exhaust the notion of correspondence. Realism survives Rorty's mockery and challenges. After we have read and understood Rorty, we can still understand Davidson's concern. The rejection of Platonic correspondism need not entail the abandonment of realism. We still have an issue.

Nonetheless, we must grant that it may be only prejudice, irrational conviction, or simple lack of understanding that makes the issue of realism appear to survive the pragmatic critique. To pursue the matter we must shift our focus to the status of our discourses and to the question of whether Rorty's pragmatism levels them in a pernicious way. In particular, we must focus on the status of scientific discourse. We now need a case in point wherein the truth of what we say constitutes a body of knowledge that may resist pragmatic reduction—if that is what it is—to a strain in conversation, and thus provide us with concrete evidence that the truth of some of our beliefs is cumulative in a way that manifests extralinguistic implications, or what must at least be deemed extralinguistic implications.

Notes

1. Consider a remark near the end of Donald Davidson's "On the Very Idea of a Conceptual Scheme" (*Proceedings of the American Philosophical Association* 17 [1973–74]: 20):

> In giving up dependence on the concept of an uninterpreted reality, something outside all schemes and science, we do not relinquish the notion of objective truth—quite the contrary.

   Not only is there a commitment to objective truth here; the burden of the paper is to show, through philosophical analysis, the incoherent nature of a set of presuppositions, and thereby to make progress through such analysis.
2. Rorty, *Consequences*, xviii.
3. Donald Davidson, "A Nice Derangement of Epitaphs," read at Queen's University, Kingston, Ontario, 27 September 1984. Forthcoming in R. Grandy and R. Warner, eds., *Philosophical Grounds of Rationality: Intentions, Categories and Ends* (Oxford: Oxford University Press).
4. For example, Rorty, *Mirror*, 259–65.
5. Rorty, *Consequences*, xviii.
6. Rorty, "Pragmatism, Davidson and Truth," 1; see also Donald Davidson, *Inquiries into Truth and Interpretation* (Oxford: Oxford University Press, 1984), xviii.
7. Rorty, "Pragmatism, Davidson and Truth", 1–2.
8. Rorty, *Mirror*, 280; see also Hilary Putnam, *Meaning and the Moral Sciences* (Cambridge: Cambridge University Press, 1978), 107–09.
9. Rorty, *Mirror*, 280.
10. James Young, "Pragmatism and the Fate of Philosophy," *Dialogue* 23 (1984): 685; see also Prado, "Rorty's Pragmatism," 441–50, and my reply to Young, C. G. Prado, "The Need for Truth," *Dialogue* 23 (1984): 687–88.
11. On his visit to Queen's University, see note 3, above.
12. Donald Davidson, "Truth and Meaning," *Synthese* 17 (1967): 304.
13. Ibid., 305.
14. Rorty, *Mirror*, 303.
15. Ibid., 258–59.

16. Ibid., 301.
17. Ibid., 304.
18. Ibid., 305. With reference to Davidson's notion of a theory of meaning, consider the following passage from Rorty, *Mirror*, 260:

> A theory of meaning, for Davidson, is not an assemblage of "analyses" of the meanings of individual terms, but rather our understanding of the inferential relations between sentences.

19. Rorty, *Consequences*, 5.
20. On the occasion of his visit to Queen's University, Kingston, Ontario, as John Milton Scott Visiting Professor, March 1985.
21. Rorty, *Consequences*, 6.
22. For instance, Rorty, *Mirror*, 309.
23. Ibid., 310–11.
24. Rorty, "Pragmatism, Davidson and Truth," 5.
25. Ibid.
26. Ibid., 29.
27. Donald Davidson, "A Coherence Theory of Truth and Knowledge," in *Kant oder Hegel?*, ed. Dieter Henrich (Stuttgart: Klett-Cotta, 1983), 436.
28. Rorty, "Pragmatism, Davidson and Truth," 19.
29. D. M. Armstrong, *A Materialist Theory of the Mind* (London: Routledge, 1968), 189–93, 204–07.
30. Davidson, "A Coherence Theory," 426.
31. Ibid., 426–27.
32. Ibid.
33. Ibid.
34. See, e.g., Rorty, *Consequences*, 90–109 and 139–59, especially 94–95, 98, and 108–09.
35. Rorty, "Cavell on Skepticism," in *Consequences*, 184–85.
36. Stanley Cavell, *The Claim of Reason: Wittgenstein, Skepticism, Morality and Tragedy* (Oxford: Clarendon Press, 1979), 236.
37. Rorty, *Consequences*, 183.
38. University of California at Berkeley, 1961; see also Stanley Cavell, *Must We Mean What We Say?* (New York: Scribner's, 1969), chapter 10.
39. Rorty, *Consequences*, 183.
40. C. G. Prado, "Hermeneutics, Analysis and the Religious," read at the 15th Congress of the International Association for the History of Religions, Sydney, Australia, August 1985.
41. Rorty, *Consequences*, 183.
42. Josef Bleicher, *Contemporary Hermeneutics: Hermeneutics as Method, Philosophy and Critique* (London: Routledge and Kegan Paul, 1980), 117.
43. Ibid., 110.
44. Ibid.
45. Ibid., 115.

46. Ibid., 116.
47. Rorty, *Mirror*, chapter 6.
48. Gadamer, *Philosophical Hermeneutics*, trans. and ed. David E. Linge (Berkeley: University of California Press, 1976), p. 31.
49. Bernstein, *Beyond Objectivism*, 168.
50. Davidson, "A Conceptual Scheme," 20.
51. See Kai Nielsen, "Scientism, Pragmatism and the Fate of Philosophy," forthcoming.
52. Rorty, *Consequences*, ibid., 14.
53. Ibid., xxiv.
54. Armstrong, *A Materialist Theory*, 206–07.
55. Hacking, "On the Frontier," 57.

Chapter 4

Objectivity, Science, and Relativism

PRELIMINARY REMARKS

My objective in this chapter is to pursue the question of whether pragmatism generally, and Rorty's pragmatism in particular, obviates concern with—and even the intelligibility of—extralinguistic truth. If we find, however, as the last chapter suggested, that we must retain some notion of extralinguistic truth—even Davidson's minimal correspondence-from-coherence one—we will conclude that pragmatism is disturbingly relativistic. As noted in the previous chapter, science provides us with a test case: even allowing for instrumentalist interpretations of scientific theories, science claims truth or objectivity at least insofar as the scientific enterprise as a whole constitutes real *progress* in intellectual inquiry, progress a Rortyan pragmatism disallows. But as I hope to show, objectivism of this sort is not necessarily the empiricist-foundationalist one which Rorty rightly rejects, but is, rather, the one Dewey accepted.

Bernstein describes objectivism as the proper contemporary contrast to relativism. In our predominantly fallibilist age, "absolutism," a view that considers Cartesian certainty attainable, is not a serious alternative to relativism. But in spite of fallibilism, there is a commitment to realism and to cumulative advancement in inquiry that is captured by the notion of scientific objectivity.

Bernstein characterizes objectivism and relativism, largely following Gadamer and Rorty, as the basic conviction that there is or must be some permanent, ahistorical matrix or framework to which we can ultimately appeal in determining the nature of rationality, knowledge, truth, reality, goodness, or rightness . . . . [R]elativism is the basic conviction that . . . in the final analysis all such concepts must be understood as relative to a specific conceptual scheme . . . form of life . . . [or] culture.[1]

This is essentially Rorty's view of objectivism. Rorty and Bernstein stress the methodological aspect, as opposed to the realist aspect that is more dominant in Davidson. Both interpret the shift away from absolutist views as only a replacement of evident truths with reliable methods for acquiring truths, as if Descartes's metaphysical conclusions, but not his rationalist methodology, had been found wanting.

I would describe objectivism somewhat differently: first, objectivism maintains that while fallibility must be acknowledged—Cartesian certainty is not attainable—it is nonetheless the world that determines true beliefs (the extralinguistic component); second, though perspectivism must also be acknowledged—there can be no neutral description—there are priorities among descriptions when means-to-ends considerations predominate, and avoidance of high-priority descriptions requires special explanation (the onus is on the methodological dissenter); third, descriptions of the highest priority with respect to means-to-ends considerations must be mutually and separately compatible with all theoretical explanations of the most general sort (Davidson's translatability thesis); fourth, high-priority means-to-ends-related descriptions are prerequisite to effective manipulative control of what is described (this is the objectivist assumption most offensive to feminists); and fifth, and most relevant to this discussion, fallibilism must be a preparedness to acknowledge that our descriptions may be superseded by better ones, where "better" means that the greater efficacy of some set of descriptions is due to more accurate rendition of some aspect of the world, an accuracy achieved through cumulative success in description and manipulation. Rather than construing objectivism as criterial and methodological reliability in virtue of truth-as-correspondence, I want to construe objectivism, in a more restricted manner, as attribution of the efficacy of theories and descriptions to greater *correctness* in our projects. This minimal objectivism is not foundationalist in the sense that we can seek—and find—epistemological grounds for what we believe, or that we can develop a methodology that will guarantee success in inquiry. But it is foundationalist in the restricted sense that the truth of some of our beliefs is grounded in how things are; that truth is not wholly intralinguistic. On this view the objectivist/relativist contrast survives, albeit in modified form.

The basic point I want to defend against Rorty is more modest than the objectivist's about universal criteria or methodologies. I want to argue only that progress in inquiry is possible in the sense that we get things more and more right as we elaborate and test hypotheses and descriptions. It may be that the complexity of the universe is such that as we progress in inquiry we find our theories increasingly restricted by an aspectival specificity. That is, getting things more and more right may mean being right about comparatively less and less. But that does not deny objectivity. Part of being more and more right about the world is coming to understand how overwhelming complexity limits correctness. The efficacy of good and better vocabularies is not absolute by virtue of being a feature of vocabularies themselves and the wealth of possibilities they offer. Rather, the efficacy of a vocabulary has to do with how well it captures how things are. We may not be able to establish descriptive accuracy directly; we cannot compare descriptions and the world, because we cannot look with wholly impartial and unconditioned eyes on the world. Nonetheless, we must *attribute* success in coping with the world to "getting things right," or at least *more* right. But this is not to say that the efficacy of a vocabulary is a function of how closely it approaches the world's own preferred language and a wholly neutral mode of description. It is, however, to judge our vocabularies and discourses as better or worse by virtue of something external to them, and so, by implication, to construe as relativistic Rorty's intralinguistic view of truth and rejection of objectivity.

Rorty thinks his rejection of objectivism is not relativistic because the objectivist/relativist distinction is discarded with scheme/content dualism. The reason is that beliefs cannot then be made relative to significantly diverse conceptual schemes. Relativism becomes innocuous, a mere acknowledgment of what Gadamer describes as our immersion in language, and objectivism takes on the aspect of a mad philosophical invention. That is why Rorty thinks he avoids relativism when he understands "better," in talking about descriptions or vocabularies, as meaning simply that the new is taken up and the old is ignored or forgotten. For him, the only reason for adopting one vocabulary and discarding another is that the adopted one enables us to do more of what we want to do—and makes it *possible* for us to do things we want to do that we could not do before. In fact, in his view objectivism prevents immersion in a new vocabulary, rather than providing criteria for its assessment, because, by (falsely) promising external criteria, it precludes real novelty. If an old vocabulary is revived, then *it* is proven better in at least some contexts; if it stays forgotten because we can do more with the new, then the new is "better." But there is no *progress* in the abandonment of one vocabulary or set of descriptions for another. This is the key to Rorty's view of science and to his difference from Dewey.

In a very recent paper, "Science as Solidarity," Rorty explicitly tells us that "Another reason for describing us as 'relativistic' is that we pragmatists drop the idea that inquiry is destined to converge to a single point."[2] The convergence Rorty denies is not only that of theories coming together in a grand general theory or ultimate truth. It is a criterial or methodological convergence that is the heart of objectivism, namely, the possibility of universal criteria for the assessment of theories, descriptions, and vocabularies—criteria that are external to any given theory, description, or vocabulary. For the objectivist the history of our vocabulary changes, from the Aristotelian to the Newtonian to the Einsteinian, is a history of more effective theorizing by virtue of honed criterial methods. Convergence in inquiry would be one where, regardless of the wealth of theories and their subject matters, there would be progress due to methodological sophistication. We would develop judgmental and justificatory criteria that would be evermore widely and reliably applicable because of past success. Rorty does not want to allow such progressive success. For him the history of vocabulary change is one of a *broadening* of our abilities. Our new vocabularies enable us to do things we could not do in the old ones, but that does not represent a gain in power due to better description; it is a gain in intellectual or descriptive possibility. The occurrence of novelty is the only value Rorty countenances in his more Nietzschean moods. Rational inquiry, or the broad intellectual enterprise, is not a project of *discovery*; it is one of *creation*, albeit often only of creative reorganization: " . . . inquiry is a matter of continually reweaving a web of beliefs rather than the application of criteria to cases."[3] When a Heidegger, or one of Harold Bloom's "strong" poets, speaks new words, when new metaphors are *added* to our vocabularies, or when a whole new vocabulary is initiated, then there is more than rearrangement, but none of these changes are better and better discernments of how things are. That is why science is only another way of coping, and not the road to mastery of the universe through accurate description. And it is why academic philosophy is pretentious: it assumes the possibility of piecemeal contribution and advancement, when the only real—the only edifying— contributions are the initiations of *new* vocabularies that precisely defy assessment in terms of the old.

The difficulty we face is saying *how* there is progress in inquiry without falling into a Platonistic or Cartesian view. This is the obverse to saying how language and belief have an extralinguistic and extradoxastic dimension of truth. In the present context, I am trying to say what needs to be said in terms of the objectivity of science. Admittedly, the matter of the precise nature of the objectivity of science is an extremely complex one. We can no longer believe theories are straightforwardly true descriptions, limnings of a universe amenable to detailed, exhaustive, and especially unproblematic mapping. The further we go into particle physics, the more metaphorical become the notions used to translate the mathematics of a theory; we understand the heuristic nature of the idea that quarks have "charm" or "color" or, more prosaic now, that an atom is a tiny universe. We also understand the biological sciences' use and need of at least marginally intentional concepts that resist reduction to the language of chemistry. Given our sophistication and the consequent fallibilism, we cannot defend a notion of objectivity as simple methodological access to a universe devoid of complicating facets. So how do we retain objectivity or realism within our sophistication? This is what I take to be Davidson's concern: the retention of realism, given a sophistication that precludes a simple correspondence view of truth.

We must decide if rejection of the scheme/content distinction does in fact render pragmatism nonrelativistic by making the objectivist/relativist contrast unintelligible. This is the same issue as whether a pragmatic, intralinguistic construal of truth makes the realist/nonrealist contrast ultimately unintelligible and forces us to admit that Davidson's notion of correspondence is innocuous and that his assertion and defense of realism is wrong. But whereas retaining some form of extralinguistic truth—even if only in Davidson's holistic way—may be difficult to differentiate from a prejudicial response to Rorty's pragmatic proposals, there may be clearer, if not more compelling, reasons for retaining objectivity—and hence extralinguistic truth—in science conceived rather minimally as a truly progressive enterprise. In addition, unlike the very abstract issue of truth, it is as important to nonphilosophers as to philosophers whether we must attribute a special status to scientific discourse, thereby acknowledging some inherent ranking among our discourses, and whether rejection of such a ranking is an enlightened move into the postphilosophical era or a denial of something real. We may, therefore, gain a little more ground here than in the consideration of truth.

RELATIVISM

As suggested earlier, the charge of nihilistic or vicious relativism is probably the most common one made against pragmatism, and it is more disturbing than charges of nonrealism. The latter are, after all, limited to philosophical assessments of the position. The former is more general and, most important, would pertain to even a *post*philosophical evaluation of a given position. To recapitulate what was said in chapter 1, pragmatism is accused of nihilism on the grounds that to reject extralinguistic truth and objectivity is to make all values equal—in effect to negate value—by denying grounding to any. In the particular case, the rejection of truth and objectivity denies the special value accorded to scientific discourse as the embodiment of objective methodology, equating that discourse with any other we find productive and, most important, denying that its productivity derives from anything outside the discourse.

In chapter 1 I spoke of two charges against pragmatism: vicious relativism and nihilism. It was useful to stress there the difference between charges of an epistemological, and of a more axiological, sort. But it is better here to show how issues of possible idealistic or nonrealist consequences to pragmatism are subsumed by the issue of whether pragmatism levels our discourses and is therefore relativistic in a vicious or nihilistic way.

The material most relevant to the issue of nihilistic relativism in Rorty's views is found mainly in *Consequences*, where there are essays that range more widely than those in *Mirror*. Much of what is scattered throughout *Consequences* is conveniently reiterated in his more recent Howison Lecture, "Relativism."[4] In that lecture Rorty approaches the issue of relativism by distinguishing between two ways "human beings try to give a sense to their lives."[5] The first is by relating one's life to a community and its practices, and the second is by attempting to relate one's life to an abstraction describable without reference to individuals or a particular community. Rorty terms the first a concern with "solidarity," the second a concern with "objectivism."[6] It is the concern with solidarity that is pragmatic. The concern with objectivism involves both correspondism and a commitment to ahistorical truths and natures.[7]

In characterizing relativism, Rorty lists three interpretations: the view that "every belief is as good as every other"; the view that "true" is equivocal; and the view that "there is nothing to be said about . . . truth or rationality apart from descriptions of the familiar procedures of justification."[8] While Rorty equates pragmatism with the third of these views, pragmatism is usually accused of incorporating the first, and this puzzles Rorty. He contends that

> the pragmatist is not holding a positive theory which says that something is relative to something else. He is . . . making the purely *negative* point that we should drop the traditional distinction between knowledge and opinion, construed as the distinction between truth as correspondence to reality and truth as a commendatory term for well-justified beliefs. The reason that the realist calls this negative claim "relativistic" is that he cannot believe that anybody would seriously deny that truth has an intrinsic nature.[9]

Rorty's strategy is to try to show how the charge of relativism is question-begging. His aim is to make out how "the pragmatist is a relativist only on realist premises."[10] Rorty's claim is that

> If one grants the realist that there is a paradigmatic sense of words like "true" which is given to them by procedures which are somehow *more* than "just the practices of a community", than [sic] it will make sense to suggest that we flag special cases in which these procedures are inapplicable. But if one does not think that there is anything permanent and trans-historical in *any* area of inquiry, then the whole question about relativism and absolutism will seem pointless.[11]

Rorty admits that the burden of proof is on the pragmatist, for there is a very long history of commitment to objectivity. (And it is interesting that Rorty acknowledges that history here, while he seems not to in the case of Davidson's concern to defeat skepticism, as we saw in the last chapter.) But acceptance of the burden of proof should not be taken as acceptance of the appropriateness of a relativistic characterization of pragmatism.

However, the required proof cannot really be that; it cannot be a demonstration consisting of arguments.[12] It can only be a *showing* of how objectivism fails, and hence how relativism loses its sense by losing its contrast. Rorty consistently attempts to defeat hostile responses to pragmatism by recharacterizing the enabling conditions for those responses in ways that he expects will reveal their incoherency, or their dependency on incoherent notions such as that of correspondence. With respect to relativism, as with respect to idealism or nonrealism, Rorty tries to deconstruct traditional presuppositions. And again, we wonder how he feels he can proceed in this manner without begging the question. Here again his treatment of Cavell provides an illuminating example.

In spite of his sharp criticism of its treatment of skepticism, Rorty thinks Cavell's *The Claim of Reason* makes an important contribution to ethics. Rorty's praise for Cavell's views on morality centers on the latter's rejection of the notion that right action is *principled* action in the sense of conforming to overriding principles external to the agent's form of life. That is, Cavell rejects the idea that morality has foundations beyond those of practice and commitment. He contends that "morality must leave itself open to repudiation; it provides *one* possibility of settling conflict."[13] More important for my present concern, he adds that "No rule or principle could function in a moral context the way regulatory or defining rules function in games."[14] Cavell rejects traditional philosophical efforts to ground morality on supreme principles that are ahistorical and external to particular forms of life. And he goes further, arguing that what philosophers have traditionally offered as grounding for morality simply would not work as intended, even if real. This is Rorty's line of attack with respect to foundationalist objectivism, for he charges that correspondence, *a priori* knowledge, or *a posteriori* evidence wholly fail as "grounds" for knowledge or operational procedures for achieving knowledge.

Rorty refers with approval to Cavell's point that philosophers seek principles underlying morality because they feel compelled to understand how morality is binding, and laments that they fail to see how appeal to rules or principles could not make morality binding without prior commitment. There should be no felt-need to explain how morality is binding, but if there is, recourse to rules and principles cannot satisfy that need, for as Cavell puts it,

> if there is a sense that something more than personal commitment is necessary, then the appeal to rules comes too late. For rules are themselves binding only subject to our commitment.[15]

What Cavell takes as sufficient is *practice*—the form of life—as does Rorty. There is no need to "ground" morality in transcendent principles or the will of a god.

The case of Cavell on morality provides an insight into how Rorty thinks of the move to foundations external to practices. The lesson here is that if in morality, where we most demand grounding principles, nothing is to be found beyond our practices, then we must come to terms with the autonomy of our practices and discourses. We must accept that, in Heideggerian terms, nothing can "save" us. *We* are the ones who establish criteria and obligation. In like manner, the cognitive enterprise of inquiry is a set of practices and discourses. The doing of science, like moral practice, *just works*. It does not work because it limns reality, because it proceeds along a secure methodology. Science does not exhibit efficacy because of anything outside itself, such as truly described states of affairs; like morality, science is not efficacious by virtue of being governed by objective principles. Rorty's approval of Cavell turns on recognition that, as noted in the previous chapter, there simply is no surety—whether in science or morality or any other practice we might want to "legitimize" by relating it to something that guarantees it from outside itself.

But the traditional philosopher will not be satisfied, nor will the layperson influenced by centuries of striving for objectivity in theoretical and practical judgments. The abandonment of objectivity will seem to them only relativization, not clarification of the nature of morality or of cognitive inquiry. Rorty must show that the pragmatist is indeed "a relativist only on realist premises." He must argue convincingly that to charge pragmatism with nihilistic or vicious relativism is to wrongly presuppose that there *must* be ahistorical, "objective" foundations for judgment, and therefore that pragmatism can only be relativistic if it denies those foundations. Rorty must expose objectivist demands as question-begging because they preclude the possibility that judgmental standards or justificatory criteria can be intralinguistic and intracultural, that without objective grounds they can still serve as standards or criteria. Rorty must show that objectivism and relativism are not exhaustive alternatives, because both presuppose what pragmatism denies, namely, the coherence of the notion of ahistorical foundations. To do so, Rorty must argue that if commitment and form of life are thought inadequate to explain moral and cognitive judgment, it must be because of a deeply confused presupposition that only transcendencies can ground morality and cognition. He must further demonstrate that if the intelligibility of such transcendencies is granted, an apparently single alternative will be generated—the relativistic position that denies those transcendencies and construes their lack as the ultimate equivalence of all values.

The trouble is that many will not think objectivist presuppositions beg the question against pragmatism. They will see them as the *conditions* of discourse about cognition and morality. Rorty's success turns again on altering perceptions of the presuppositions at issue; he must bring about a shift of perspective.

One can attempt the shift in perspective by following Cavell's Wittgensteinian point that moral rules or principles simply cannot work as they are required to work. The deconstructive argument is that just as rules and principles cannot "ground" morality because they presuppose commitment and an impetus to apply them, neither can objectivity and correspondence be *grounds* for inquiry, because to be so they would have to be accessible, and they are conceived as precisely *in*accessible. Once rules and principles fail as the grounds of morality, they cease to be the sorts of things that are applied at all, and become simply *descriptive* of a form of life. In a similar way, objectivity and correspondence are attainable only intralinguistically, so our methodological and justificatory procedures are descriptions of our forms of life, not avenues from belief and language to an "objective" world. Showing that objectivist presuppositions and demands are misconceived and self-defeating is the heart of Rorty's general polemic against foundationalism, of his rejection of the traditional philosophic commitment to " . . . the possibility of *grounding* the European form of life—of showing it to be . . . more than a contingent human project."[16]

Rorty's antifoundationalism is motivated by a need for intellectual openness, which is evident in his view that the " . . . *moral* task of the philosopher or the cultural critic is to defend the openness of human conversation against all those temptations and real threats that seek closure."[17] And this is just one way in which all cognitive judgments are unavoidably normative. The temptations to closure are conceptual as well as, say, political. Rorty maintains that foundationalist presuppositions impose closure to the extent that they discourage questioning of their own grounds and restrict novelty by promising evaluative criteria external to any discourse. But the fear of foundationalist closure seems to cause a glossing of the difference between, on the one hand, the empiricist foundationalism we have had since Descartes and the Rationalist *a priorism* we have had since Kant and, on the other hand, a Davidsonian position which, in allowing room for holistic correspondence, allows room for some

form of non-Cartesian objectivity—at least of the sort that in turn permits
real progress in inquiry across cultural and linguistic boundaries.

The trouble is that, just as correspondism is equated with Platonic
correspondism, Rorty equates objectivism with Rationalist and/or empiricist foundationalism. That is, he disallows that we might give a *non*foundationalist sense to objectivity. He disallows that cognitive inquiry (and
moral practice) might have extralinguistic and extracultural dimensions
that are neither correspondence-guaranteed, *a priori* transcendent foundations nor *a posteriori* elemental evidencies.

Bernstein distinguishes between Rorty's metacritique of philosophy and
his endorsement of pragmatism, and in that way allows the critical part of
its full weight without necessarily accepting the positive pragmatic proposals. Comparing Rorty with Bernstein brings out how both express a
deep commitment to *dialogue*; how both think rationality and value need to
be reconceived in terms that avoid both the objectivist presupposition that
the authority of rationality and value must be grounded in ahistorical
truth, and the relativist counter-claim that because diverse rationalities
and value-systems are relative to groups or forms of life, they are all
ultimately equal. Both Rorty and Bernstein want rationality and value
recognized as dialogical, and progress as consensual. With respect to
relativism Rorty contends that

> the real issue is not between people who think one view is as good as
> another and people who do not. It is between those who think our
> culture, or purpose, or intuitions cannot be supported except conver-
> sationally, and people who still hope for other sorts of support.[18]

As noted above, Rorty wants us to acknowledge that we are on our own.
But he wants us to understand that to recognize we are on our own is not
to embrace relativism or nihilism—if for no other reason than that
Davidson has deprived us of the contrast we need to be relativists. We are
supposed to realize that we must be content with the "Socratic virtues."
As Bernstein puts it,

> The heart of [Rorty's] pragmatism is a defense of the Socratic virtues:
> "willingness to talk, to listen to other people, to weigh the conse-

quences of our actions upon other people." But according to Rorty, "These are *simply* moral virtues," and there is no metaphysical or epistemological guarantee of success . . . . Nietzsche . . . helped us to see that there is no "metaphysical comfort" to be found that grounds or secures these virtues.[19]

It is not only truth-as-correspondence that we must forgo; we must forgo *anything* outside our practices. This message, seen from the perspective of the philosophical tradition, is as old as Protagoras; it is relativism. But some, like Bernstein, think it may be a new message—one that may herald a new conception of rationality, and hence of the methodology and criteria the traditional philosopher is so anxious to protect against Rorty's critique. Bernstein provides a "best possible case" for how to read what Rorty is up to, because he construes Rorty's critique, if not his more positive proposals, as part of a general, ongoing overhaul of our conception of rationality and as a sharp reappraisal of the distinctions philosophers have relied on for so long.

THE EVAPORATION OF RELATIVISM

Bernstein tries in *Beyond Objectivism and Relativism* to examine the ways a number of recent thinkers have initiated what he considers a reconception of rationality. Bernstein discusses Thomas Kuhn, Paul Feyerabend, Peter Winch, Clifford Geertz, and others, but his major focus is on Gadamer, and, to a somewhat lesser extent, Jurgen Habermas, Rorty, and Hannah Arendt. Bernstein treats these thinkers insightfully and supports his arguments with judiciously selected quotations. He is also critical and perceptive with respect to difficulties and troubling implications. In the case of Gadamer he brings out how little we are told about truth; in the discussion of Habermas he echoes Rorty's concerns about lingering foundationalism. Bernstein even points out correctly that Rorty's reading of Dewey is problematic because he overlooks Dewey's overestimation of science, which contrasts with Rorty's own literary inclinations; and that he has not followed Dewey in practical involvement in socio-political projects.

The synoptic point of Bernstein's enterprise is that in the past several decades foundationalist philosophizing has been challenged, if not superseded, by a more dialogical way of thinking. The rise of hermeneutics is the obvious case in point. In spite of its inherent difficulties, hermeneutical thinking is coming to be preferred to "analytic" thinking of the foundationalist sort. Bernstein pleads for dialogue, for patience in conversation, for flexibility in interpretation. The move beyond objectivism and relativism is arguably a new vocabulary in Rorty's sense. It is an invitation to accept that objectivism is untenable, and that it alone makes relativism an intelligible position. Like Rorty, Bernstein wants us to see that when we abandon objectivism, relativism evaporates. In place of these two philosophical extremes we will have *conversation*.

Bernstein thinks the drive for objectivism is a product of "Cartesian Anxiety," the felt-need for certainty.[20] But he also thinks the work of the thinkers he reviews shows that there now is a "growing sense that there may be nothing—not God, Philosophy, Science, or Poetry—that satisfies our longing for ultimate foundations."[21] Bernstein concludes *Beyond Objectivism and Relativism* by saying that

> the questioning of the Either/Or of objectivism or relativism and the attempt to exorcise the Cartesian Anxiety are motivated by a practical-moral concern . . . . We can no longer share Marx's theoretical certainty or revolutionary self-confidence. There is no guarantee, there is no necessity, no "logic of history" that must inevitably lead to dialogical communities that embrace all of humanity . . . . If anything, we have . . . learned how much the contemporary world conspires against it and undermines it. And yet it is still a *telos* . . . deeply rooted in our human project.[22]

Rorty articulates the lack of guarantees more harshly:

> . . . there is nothing deep down inside us except what we have put there ourselves, no criterion that we have not created in the course of creating a practice, no standard of rationality that is not an appeal to such a criterion, no rigorous argumentation that is not obedience to our own conventions.[23]

Both Rorty and Bernstein have a deep commitment to the intellectual analog of *laissez faire* optimism or economic individualism. I do not intend this as a dark Marxist comment. What I mean is that, while recognizing the problems we generate for ourselves, both thinkers believe that dialogue and compromise, exploration of, and patience with, one another's views and needs, will make things *better*; that free trade in a marketplace of ideas is preferable to intellectual control through the imposition of sacrosanct principles or standards. Bernstein's is perhaps the more sanguine perspective, in that he seems to think dialogue is all we need, while Rorty seems to believe continuance of conversation is all we can hope for. But both are clear that there can be no appeal to anything beyond our practices. In at least this sense, both have appropriated pragmatism. There is nothing deep down inside, or in the heavens above, that can back up our values, methodologies, or justificatory practices.

But can artful articulation of the above points be enough? John Caputo has perhaps best expressed the concern that the foregoing "all we can hope for" is reductive in the sense that Rortyan conversation seems to come to *just* talk.[24] Caputo criticizes Rorty's reading of Heidegger as overly focused on the critical aspects of the latter's work, and claims that "In the end we get from Rorty neither Heideggerian 'thought' nor Gadamerian 'hermeneutics', but . . . Derrida's play of signs."[25] Caputo maintains that Rorty not only disallows Heidegger's "retrieval" of philosophy but also cuts hermeneutics off from tradition and the world by not letting it come "to grips with its own Being-in-the-world."[26] Caputo sees in Rorty's emphasis on discourse the loss of both method and grounding in Being. And there is a significant point of contact here between Caputo's complaints and Davidson's concern with defeating skepticism. Caputo feels that even if one adopts holism over correspondism and foundationalism, as he admits Heidegger did in his later work, there is still need for philosophizing about how the whole of belief may be thought to relate to the world, and this requires philosophical method, as opposed to simple diversity of discourse.

> For Heidegger the end of [foundationalist] philosophy poses the "task of thinking" (die Aufgabe des Denkens), of a meditative openness to a matter which has been progressively concealed yet . . . present in the history of metaphysics. The task of thinking is hermeneutics: to heed the message which Being ambiguously sends . . . . But for Rorty that is a . . . "pathetic" attachment . . . to the old philosophy. . . . [Rortyan] hermeneutics seeks only to recognize the plurality of discourses and is content to keep a civil conversation going.[27]

Nor is Caputo simply a disgruntled foundationalist. Whatever the relation of belief and language to "Being" or the world, it is not, in Caputo or Heidegger, a relation of simple correspondence or "grounding." And there is substance to the charge that Rorty has leveled discourses. Certainly Rorty explicitly denies that there is any *privileged* discourse that somehow better captures how things are.[28] He even attempts to erode the distinction between factual and fictional discourses, as well as that between scientific and literary discourses.[29]

Perhaps what is most disturbing about Rorty's views is not that they disallow Heideggerian talk of Being, but that the denial of absolute distinctions between discourses seems to be a denial of relative distinctions among them as well. We might come to understand how in some deep sense there is no ultimate difference between scientific and literary discourse, or even between factual and fictional discourse, but it is difficult to accept that there are not important differences between them. Of course Rorty would not *deny* those differences, but the trouble is that it is not altogether clear either on what terms or to what degree he can allow them.

Another oddity arises when we wonder how Rorty can deal with relative differences among discourses without giving away too much. The pragmatic message seems to be self-defeating in that its articulation of the point that no discourse derives a privileged status from something external to it seems to lend substance to relativism—contrary to Rorty's claim that pragmatism empties relativism of content. In this the pragmatic message is as dangerous as Davidson's avowals of realism are judged to be by Rorty. If asserting realism invites skepticism and presupposes unfortunate epistemological distinctions, then emphasizing the autonomy of discourses at least invites lamentation for objectivity and foundations, and in so doing indirectly articulates some sort of relativism, though not necessarily one involving conceptual schemes to which beliefs are relative. Rorty may answer that the notions of objectivity and correspondence, confused though they are, are *already* in place, and that his object is to defeat them. But I think the implication then is that the pragmatic perspective would ideally be an unreflective one. This idea is very hard to accept.

Though it will undoubtedly look like foundationalist thinking, our reservation can be expressed as follows: Assuming obvious differences in productivity are acknowledged, for example, between scientific and literary discourses, the pressing question concerns how they differ; by what criteria is one more productive? This recalls Kuhn's need to know why science works at all and why it works so consistently. It seems inevitable that discourses will be thought to differ by virtue of truth or better grounding.

The Rortyan response is, as we have seen, that discourses do not differ because of something *else*; they differ in being more or less productive discourses. But Rorty will add that the "obviousness" of productivity differences may be challenged. It will be pointed out that "productivity" is as problematic and perspective-centered a notion as any other.

Both of these responses prompt Caputo's claim that Rorty ends up with just talk. The first, that discourses need not be productive because of something beyond themselves, leads us to feel that to be unable to explain efficacy in terms of truth or objectivity leaves us unable to understand the judgment that a discourse is productive. We want a *theoretical* answer, one that explains productivity in terms of something not contained in the discourse. The second response, that judgments of greater productivity are themselves parts of discourses, that, to paraphrase a remark of Rorty's, they are just stories in a new vocabulary about an old vocabulary, seems question-begging. To be told that judging a discourse more productive than another is itself only a move within a discourse seems no more than a restatement of what is at issue.

Rorty's answer to Caputo must be that being left only with discourses, with conversation, is not being left with *just* talk, because we have been deprived of nothing but a philosophical fiction. That is, the phrase "just talk" has the requisite force only if we tolerate the contrast Rorty wants to extirpate, namely, that between a discourse and its "ground." The parallel with the rejection of the enabling conditions of the nonrealism charge is exact, as is the parallel with the rejection of relativism generally.

But Caputo's charge can be reformulated. As suggested above, reformulation might begin with a more careful description of what Rorty actually rejects. As we saw when we distinguished between Platonic and Davidsonian correspondism, Rorty's characterization of what he rejects is problematic. And, as indicated, it seems that objectivism is now being construed as exhausted by empiricist foundationalism.

SCIENCE

I shall now consider Bernard Williams's criticism of Rorty on the status of science, which articulates the most telling points against Rorty's attempt to deny science a privileged status. Williams's review of *Consequences* is critical of Rorty in much the same way as Caputo's article.[30] And neither is exceptional. Other thinkers have articulated their resistance to Rorty's work in similar terms.[31] Williams's criticism is important because, like Bernstein, he has clearly understood Rorty's project. Other critics, such as Charles Taylor and Donald Mannison, have in my estimation somewhat missed the point of what Rorty is up to.[32]

Williams, beginning with a quote from Rorty, characterizes Rorty's position as follows:

> "It is impossible to step outside our skins—the traditions, linguistic and other, within which we do our thinking and self-criticism—and compare ourselves with something absolute." That is one of Rorty's central theses. Or . . . it is several theses. The least contentious is that we cannot think about the world without describing it in some way . . . . [But] Rorty's pragmatism . . . reaches much more drastic conclusions . . . and claims (so it seems) that all we can ever do is compare one description with another . . . . He does not think that we can say anything substantial about the purposes served by our descriptions, against which we might test them.[33]

This characterization captures Rorty's central contention that all assessment and justification is intralinguistic, that there is neither correspondence nor foundations of any other sort in which to ground our discourses and judgments, including the scientific.

Williams locates a weakness of Rorty's position in its failure to see that claims about the status of scientific discourse are not only a matter of philosophical perspectives and presuppositions, but are also due to the nature of the scientific enterprise. That is, Williams thinks Rorty has failed to appreciate that the objectivity claimed by science, and the construal of its productivity as grounded in something beyond the discourse itself, are not simply putative philosophical mistakes. They are in part inherent in scientific discourse and in part derivative of that discourse. Williams here pinpoints an important way in which Rorty's reading of objectivism as empiricist-foundationalist fails to describe adequately our contemporary scientific enterprise. Williams notes that

> it is an important feature of modern science . . . that it makes some contribution to explaining how science itself is possible, and how

creatures that have the origins and characteristics it says we have can understand a world that has the properties it says the world has.[34]

This feature is very much at odds with a view of scientific discourse as one more discourse among many. Williams grants that "limitless numbers" of alternative scientific theories could deal with the same subject matter, but thinks the differences among those theories would be trivial or notational. And those theories would then not differ in the crucial respect that objectivity derives "from within scientific reflection itself."[35]

The Rortyan response to Williams, of course, is that he has not identified anything about the scientific discourse that forces us to accept its objectivist claims. Rorty insists that "the only sense in which science is exemplary is that it is a model of human solidarity."[36] In fact, Rorty claimed in conversation that he did not see the force of Williams's contentions or find an argument in the review. Scientific discourse may incorporate claims to objectivity, just as traditional theistic discourse holds its object to be a transcendent, omnipotent entity, but nothing about the nature of intradiscourse claims can establish such claims.

However, a crucial difference between the two cases indicates the unique status of scientific discourse. The difference is at least twofold. First, religion includes claims to objectivity and truth, but all it offers to explicate the nature of those claims is divine inspiration, which is, of course, one of the things at issue in its claim. Religion, then, only claims the objective truth of certain propositions—or at least credal religion does. Against this, it is precisely Williams's point that science does offer reflective analyses of the nature of its efficacy and so its objectivity. Second, science's claims about its own objectivity are irresistibly forceful because science can claim a degree, kind, and consistency of productivity that religious and other discourses cannot.

The key to scientific discourse's special productivity is predictability—and its corollary, repeatable testability. The special productivity of scientific discourse is most evident in the breadth and precision of its predictive and manipulative power. And it is just here that Rorty seems to run into difficulties, for he is unwilling to recognize the *cumulative* progress we have made through the formulation of hypotheses and attendant predictions and testing of predictions. In a passage that raises the question of the power of scientific discourse and underlines the point made in chapter 2 about how Rorty plays down Dewey's estimation of scientific method, Williams again quotes Rorty and characterizes his attitude toward science:

"Pragmatism . . . does not erect Science as an idol . . . . It views science as one genre of literature—or, put the other way around, literature and the arts as inquiries on the same footing as scientific inquiries . . . ." In a similar vein [Rorty] says . . . that it simply turned out that the Galilean picture of the universe worked better than, say, an Aristotelian picture.[37]

To say it simply *turns out* that one vocabulary proves more effective than another is to express Rorty's conviction that no discourse, no enterprise, is efficacious because of special connectedness to anything outside itself. And even though he readily admits that language has causal connections to the world, those connections apparently cannot be traded on in justificatory projects—leaving us puzzled about what Rorty's causal admission comes to.

Williams thinks that in adopting the attitude toward science that it is only one more narrative we use to cope, Rorty conflates two questions: one about the nature of the success of science, and one about whether its successful methods provide derivable guidelines for future success. Williams thinks Rorty is right to dismiss the second as answerable only with platitudes, but he thinks something can be said about real progress with respect to the first, and that such progress can only be "finding out what the world is really like."[38]

It might be argued that Rorty only wants us to jettison ideas about science as better description of the world *knowable* as better description. But he certainly speaks and writes as if he wants us to accept that scientific discourse—like any other discourse—is productive in some autonomous sense. Rorty wants to think of doing science as coping, not as an enterprise that is successful at capturing how things really are, and that sounds to Williams as if Rorty wants us to accept a kind of discourse-idealism that attributes productivity to descriptions or discourses in their own right. This point emerges clearly in the way Williams construes Rorty's admission that the vocabularies of science have "power." Williams asks, "They have power or success in doing what?"[39] Williams answers his own question by saying that Rorty is "rash" enough to claim that the power of science's vocabularies resides in generating predictions. But that must mean generating *better* predictions than alternative discourses.

It is the possible sense or force of "better" that puzzles Williams:

Doesn't "better" mean, for instance, "true"? On Rorty's view there is no point in getting off at that stop: "Truth is simply a compliment paid to sentences seen to be paying their way." But what is it that we see when we see that they are paying their way?[40]

But, to paraphrase remarks made in discussion, Rorty thinks "better" just means doing something new; "better" is when the new is taken up and the old is forgotten. The story of progress is the narrative told in the new vocabulary about the old vocabulary.[41]

In Rorty's view, recognizing the productivity of a description or an entire discourse is a matter of judging that it is getting us what we want. It is not a matter of judging that the description or discourse is getting us what we want better than *any* alternative; it is only judging that it is doing so better than some previously used alternative. The latter comparison raises no theoretical problems, for it is a judgment about one description or discourse from the point of view of another, and one made in light of objectives that encompass both alternative descriptions or discourses. What Rorty is on guard against is the "hard" objectivist claim that we can make similar judgments *in the abstract*, that we can judge kinds of descriptions or discourses as better or worse in a general way, outside particular contexts and without reference to either particular objectives, competing descriptions, or discourses.

In response to the qualified objectivism I described, which maintains that real progress in inquiry is discernible after the fact, Rorty can press the point that the productivity of science is itself part of an elaborate story or construal, but this looks too much like begging the question. The response is especially unsuccessful against the persistence of what underlies Williams's critique, namely, recognition of how science incorporates an understanding of its own objectivity. The scientific story of progress is *not* just another narrative, because it includes description of processes by which success has built on success—even across radical perspectival and theoretical shifts—and of the crucial self-corrective role of duplication of experimental effort. The change between Newton and Einstein may well have consisted of the adoption of a new vocabulary, but Williams points out that the new vocabulary is not a *discontinuous* one because it must incorporate the old. That sort of cumulative continuity, if not progress, does not lend itself to being understood as Rorty wants it understood. He sees scientific revolutions as wholesale changes of metaphors. Nor can Rorty dismiss the assimilation of yesterday's science by today's as simple

Whiggishness, for that assimilation involves very detailed accommodation and translation of old theory into new theory.

Williams thinks Rorty is denying or ignoring the achievement in science of a kind of objectivity that need not be identified with foundationalism or truth-as-correspondence, but that still belies the alleged equality among discourses. Williams's main point against Rorty is that the current view of scientific discourse—as productive because of *some* sort of accurate representation—is a well-grounded product of scientific method and conception, not the result of allegedly mistaken philosophical views. The force of this is that the objectivity of scientific discourse is not something foisted on it by philosophers, and therefore is not amenable to retraction or dismissal by philosophical argument. It is not up to the philosopher to relieve the scientist of objectivity in science, because the objectivity science achieves is an integral *product* of the scientific enterprise.

Rorty does not—or will not—see that the scientific discourse is a special discourse because of features not amenable to intellectual reconstrual. To put the point in Rortyan terms, we cannot encompass the scientific narrative in a broader narrative, and thereby make the scientific just another story. This is because the scientific enterprise is part narrative and part practice, and the practice part produces something new that we might call retrospective objectivity, which facilitates real progress in inquiry. I think this is just where the gap between Dewey and Rorty becomes most evident. Dewey recognized the special nature of inquiry in endorsing Peirce's notion that inquiry inevitably leads to real progress—a notion Rorty explicitly rejects. And while it may be argued that Rorty rejects only the assertion that inquiry *inevitably* leads to real progress, the disagreement persists because Dewey and Peirce thought that scientific method did lead eventually to pragmatic truth as the convergence of inquiry.[42] As Williams notes, Rorty thinks Galilean science just happened to be more productive than Aristotelian science. He clearly denies a progression between the two; he is committed to seeing the shift from one to the other as radically discontinuous. I doubt that Dewey or Peirce could have accepted the degree of contingency in inquiry, or the "best" use of intelligence, for which Rorty argues. Both Dewey and Peirce clearly believed in progress, in getting things *right*, even though not by fashioning true linguistic portraits of an epistemologically distant world. This difference is not, of course, a conclusive point against Rorty, but it does bring out how even classical pragmatism did not dismiss real progress in inquiry.

To sum up, then, I think Williams is correct in charging that Rorty runs together the question of the nature of scientific success and the question of objectivity as a recipe for guaranteeing *future* success. We do not want to be objectivists in the latter sense; we do not want to claim that we can discern a methodology for the certain achievement of truth. But we want to be objectivists in the more modest sense I outlined earlier and grant that we can retrospectively discern progress of a real sort, at least in scientific inquiry. I do not think we can understand how science could turn out to be efficacious if it were simply an autonomous discourse; I do not think we can accept that we might be provided with a new and radically different vocabulary that would let us *forget* science. This preclusion is just the sort Rorty most decries, for it is an imposed rational limitation that disallows further invention in a given area. But I see no way of avoiding this point: Whatever new vocabulary might somehow displace science would have to accommodate its progressive achievements and the internal structure that has facilitated those achievements. Science has carried us to plausible speculation about the first moments of the existence of the universe. What underlies that progression cannot simply be jettisoned with an outmoded vocabulary. It outstrips in kind the structures that supported vocabularies we *have* forgotten, such as those of the Greek myths and phrenology. And any accommodation by a new vocabulary to the structure of the present scientific enterprise must amount to a *de facto* continuity. In other words, I am not arguing that we cannot allow a new vocabulary, only that science cannot now be wholly displaced by a radically new vocabulary—and that is to say it has made real progress.

We must conclude that, while our retention of truth, even though of a Davidsonian sort, might still be question-begging against Rorty, we have something quite different in the case of scientific objectivity. Scientific objectivity—of the retrospective sort—is not something we *retain*; in the face of Rorty's contentions, it is a given that demands explanation. The history of science will not accommodate itself to the dimensions of just another story. This does not establish that science sententially replicates the universe or employs a fail-safe methodology. It establishes that science has accrued both a consistent record of prediction and control that defies attribution to some sort of absolute or autonomous efficacy, and the breadth of possibility of a delineable discourse. This last point is important, too, because Rorty often sounds as if he thinks vocabularies, metaphor-sets, and discourses constitute markedly distinct units. In fact, the only thing that prevents him from characterizing such vocabularies or discourses as diverse conceptual schemes is his adamant denial of the meaningfulness of radical conceptual-scheme diversity.

We have, then, another modest conclusion. Not only does it seem that the issue of truth is still with us, it also seems that the scientific enterprise resists denial of objectivity, at least in the sense of retrospective acknowledgment of real progress. But these conclusions, rather than justifying dismissal of Rorty's claims, prompt us to ask what he can have in mind in arguing as he does. In the next chapter I will pursue the issues raised in this and previous chapters, with a view to making some positive proposals.

Notes

1. Bernstein, *Beyond Objectivism*, 8.
2. Rorty, "Science as Solidarity," 7a.
3. Ibid., 6.
4. Richard Rorty, "Relativism," the Howison Lecture, University of California at Berkeley, 31 January 1983.
5. Ibid., 1.
6. Ibid.
7. Consider the following passage from "Science as Solidarity," 6:

> Philosophers who . . . wish to ground solidarity in objectivity . . . have to construe truth as correspondence to reality . . . . By contrast, we pragmatists, who wish to reduce objectivity to solidarity, do not require either a metaphysics or an epistemology.

   Consider also Rorty's remark from the same lecture that "Worry about . . . 'objectivity' [is] characteristic of a secularized culture in which the scientist replaces the priest." One of my students, Andrew Young, articulating his puzzlement about what to do with our present notion of objectivity, commented that to try to ground the efficacy of our scientific discourse now was like trying to figure out what to do with confession once the priests were gone.
8. Ibid., 7.
9. Ibid., 8.
10. Ibid., 13.
11. Ibid.
12. The pragmatist can neither accept the enabling conditions for objectivity claims, in order to defeat them on their own terms, nor contend that her arguments are demonstrations. The only alternative is a combination of deconstructive persuasion, with respect to the enabling conditions, and the proffering of a more productive alternative. See, for example, Rorty, *Consequences*, xxvi, 156.
13. Cavell, *The Claim of Reason*, 269.

14. Ibid., 307.
15. Ibid.
16. Rorty, *Consequences*, 172.
17. Bernstein, *Beyond Objectivism*, 205.
18. Rorty, *Consequences*, 167.
19. Bernstein, *Beyond Objectivism*, 198.
20. See ibid., 16–25.
21. Ibid., 230.
22. Ibid., 230–31.
23. Rorty, *Consequences*, xlii.
24. Caputo, "The Thought of Being."
25. Ibid., 662.
26. Ibid., 678.
27. Ibid., 665.
28. See, e.g., Rorty, *Mirror*, 373–79; and Rorty, *Consequences*, 162, 163, 165, 193, 195, 198. Consider especially the passage on 199:

> When Galileo came up with his mathematicized vocabulary, he was successfully concluding an inquiry which was, in the only sense I can give the term, hermeneutical. The same goes for Darwin. I do not see any interesting differences between what they were doing and what biblical exegetes, literary critics, or historians of culture do.

29. See Rorty, "Is There a Problem about Fictional Discourse?", in *Consequences*, 110–38, especially 127–30.
30. Bernard Williams, "Auto-da-Fe," *New York Review*, 28 April 1983.
31. See works referred to in note 11, chapter 1. See also, for example, J. N. Mohanty, "Rorty, Phenomenology and Transcendental Philosophy," *Journal of the British Society for Phenomenology* 14 (1983); Chris Murphy, Critical Notice of *Mirror*, *Australasian Journal of Philosophy* 59 (1981); Robert Schwartz, Review of *Mirror*, *The Journal of Philosophy* 80 (1983); Quentin Skinner, "The End of Philosophy?", *New York Review*, 19 March 1981.
32. Charles Taylor, "Understanding in Human Sciences," *Review of Metaphysics* 34 (1980): 25–38, and Rorty's reply, ibid., 39–46, as well as Taylor's response, ibid., 47–49, 52–55. A somewhat more appreciative, but still critical, treatment is Taylor's review of *Mirror*, "Minerva through the Looking Glass," *Times Literary Supplement*, 26 December 1980. See also Donald Mannison, Review of *Consequences*, *Australasian Journal of Philosophy* 63 (1983).
33. Williams, "Auto-da-Fe."
34. Ibid.
35. Ibid.
36. Rorty, "Science as Solidarity," 8; consider also the passage on page 4:

> What I am calling "pragmatism" might also be called "left-wing Kuhnianism". It has also been rather endearingly called (by . . . Clark Glymour)

"the new fuzziness", because it is an attempt to blur just those distinctions between the objective and the subjective and between fact and value which the criterial conception of rationality has developed. We fuzzies would like to substitute the idea of "unforced agreement" for that of "objectivity".

37. Williams, "Auto-da-Fe."
38. Ibid.
39. Ibid.
40. Ibid.
41. On the occasion of his visit to Queen's University as the John Milton Scott visiting lecturer, 23 and 24 January 1986.
42. Dewey, *Logic*, 345n.

Chapter 5

Pragmatism and Progress

PRELIMINARY REMARKS

This chapter addresses indirectly the question of whether philosophy can continue—if not as the adjudicator of reason, then as a discipline that can still criteriologically encompass other disciplines while having some subject matter peculiar to itself. The relevant example of such subject matter is skeptical doubts, and Davidson's concern about how we might respond to them. This question is part of the general question about progress in inquiry, or the growth of knowledge, and both are raised not only by Rorty's particular critique, but also by the increasingly historicized nature of intellectual reflection. As I mentioned in chapter 1, Rorty articulates in a provocative manner developments that are fairly evident: just those developments, in fact, that Bernstein construes as a change in the nature of rationality.

We can raise the question of philosophy's survival in several ways: we might ask whether philosophy can be recalled from Rortyan banishment—say, in the form of the current "applied philosophy"; whether transcendental arguments can be vindicated or refurbished; whether Rorty's polemics are themselves essentially philosophical arguments, as Taylor suggests in his review of *Mirror*; or whether Davidson's assertion of realism, and hence his continuation of philosophy, inescapably illustrates the viability of philosophy against Rorty's dismissals.[1] But the more pressing issue concerns what we are to say about progress in inquiry *generally*, and here science is a better case in point than philosophy. Having tried to show how the issues of truth and progress in inquiry persist in spite of Rorty's contentions, I want now to offer a recapitulary overview of Rorty and an amplification of the progress-in-inquiry issue.

113

What should be clear from the preceding chapters is that Rorty does not intend his position to be a philosophically revisionary one. In fact, Rorty considers himself at odds with the revisionary philosophical tradition. In this he is like Hume, seeing himself as a champion of the mundane against philosophical reconstruction. Rorty views philosophical—read "correspondist and foundationalist"—theories as hopelessly arcane reconstruals of the ordinary things we say and do. He wants to bring out how philosophical revisions are misguidedly presented as "clarifications" of the mundane, as articulations of what allegedly underlies our common practices. In the case of truth, our commendation of sentences that "pay their way" is made out by philosophers as crypto-assertion of correspondence between those sentences and facts; in the case of justificatory practices and value, expressions of correctness, desire, or esteem are seen to make tacit reference to ahistorical principles or objective worth.[2] Even more like Wittgenstein than like Hume, Rorty is engaging in philosophical therapy, trying to lead us out of theory-bred confusions. If there is to be revision, it must be edifying revision: the provision of new paradigms, of new *genres*; the initiation of new practices.[3] But any of these will be *new*; they will not be merely a sharper discernment, discovery, or better enactment of something ahistorical and previously only inadequately understood.

In Rorty's view, the traditional philosopher, driven by Cartesian Anxiety, has inevitably tried to discern ahistorical "conceptual" or even metaphysical infrastructures in our sayings and practices. And the spars and girders of those infrastructures have been thought to be anchored in something independent of sayings and practices: The World, Truth, Value. Rorty's concern is to show the pointlessness of such efforts, and to indicate how what philosophers actually do is erect fantastic structures. His aim, then, can hardly be to offer alternative infrastructures. Nor does he see himself proposing something edifying. Rorty seems genuinely not to picture himself as a latter-day Dewey or Heidegger. Rather, he thinks of himself as only putting traditional philosophy in general, and analytic philosophy in particular, in their place—their historical and historicist place. His work is intended to expose the obfuscations and pretensions of academic philosophy. He is irked by charges of relativism and nonrealism, characterizing them as question-begging and misconceived in that they are directed at *philosophical* claims. He regards his polemics not as so much more philosophy, but as a critique of a long tradition of rather fruitless intellectual activity—one exposed as fruitless by Nietzsche, Dewey, Wittgenstein, and Heidegger.

Rorty deplores the mirror imagery of traditional philosophy. In his view, the traditional philosopher, obsessed by the felt-need for certainty and foundations, takes the structures of our beliefs and practices, including language, and construes those structures as congruent with the structure of reality, and therefore able to facilitate the acquisition of reliable belief-content and of referential success. The structural congruence is called "Rationality" or "correspondence," depending on whether we are interested in our capacity to mirror logical or empirical reality in consciousness or the ideational and propositional portraits that constitute the mirroring.

Strikingly enough, this looking glass epistemological view, which claims to explain our dependable awareness of the world, has some worrisome consequences for value. If consciousness is a mirroring of the world, and therefore separate from the world, then value appears to be too much a part of consciousness. And if value is to be as important as it seems to be, it must be made independent of consciousness. Value must be made objective; it must be projected into the world. This is accomplished by taking valu*ing* also as portrayal, as an image in consciousness of some aspect of objective worth, of Value itself.

Rorty thinks that with respect to both truth and value, the thought underlying the philosophical tradition is thoroughly Cartesian. The traditional philosopher's thinking is that belief, language, and the intentional aspects of practices, as images of the world in the mirror of nature, are not really *of* the world. As functions of consciousness they must be somehow externally related to the world in ways that need to be traced, justified, and explained. Consciousness is deemed qualitatively different from the world, and so in need of being somehow connected to the world. And of course the connection is then itself in need of assessment for accuracy.

Rorty does not want to see consciousness isolated and made into only a mirror of nature. He thinks consciousness is part of nature, and that truth and value are activities of that particular part of nature. He sees no need to justify or legitimize the relation of consciousness to nature by grounding its contents in something supposedly stable and authoritative. Such attempts to ground what we say, do, and believe lead inexorably to confusion, for what we believe, do, and say always overflow the restrictions imposed by theoretical grounding. We then have to gerrymander large chunks of our activities to fit our theories. We end up, for instance, inventing negative facts, or "subsistence," to explain what we say about books not on shelves and about some characters in books.

But the problem facing Rorty is how to say all of this in a way that does not sound revisionary in the sense of being an alternative philosophical position. In particular, he must avoid construal of his position as relativistic. Rorty responds to charges of nihilistic relativism by undercutting the conditions that make those charges possible. His objective is twofold: to show the charges as question-begging, and to better illustrate the nature of what is being debunked. Showing the charges to be question-begging is largely a deconstructive enterprise, a matter of showing how to accuse someone of relativism is to presuppose the viability of the distinction between objectivism and relativism, which is in turn—against all appearances—to effectively conceive objectivism as unachievable and relativism as inevitable. Rorty tries to show that objectivism must be rejected because it requires that we somehow get out of language and belief— perhaps through *a priori* knowledge or divine inspiration. It should then be clear that relativism, lacking a contrast, is not a position at all.

If relativism is construed as the only (lamentable) alternative to impossible objectivism, if the need to get out of language and belief, to have access to indubitable foundations, is even tacitly accepted, then *remaining* within language and belief must be perceived as a very unfortunate epistemic condition. That condition is then called "relativism" or "coherentism" or "idealism," and there is much philosophical gnashing of teeth at the desperateness of the plight it entails, namely, an inability to know *how things really are*. On this scheme, Rorty's antifoundationalism and anticorrespondism must look like pernicious relativism. But he wants only to persuade us that there is no contrast to the notion of being limited to language and belief, so that efforts to get out of language and belief, or lamentations of our "imprisonment," are foolish.

The second part of Rorty's objective—the illustration of the nature of the presuppositions at issue—is the most Wittgensteinian. It is primarily therapeutic, for its point is that once what is presupposed is fully understood, it is seen as unworkable. The case in point is correspondence. Once it is recognized that establishing correspondence, or even making out the notion, requires the comparison of language to the world from *outside* language, correspondence will be exposed as impossible and therefore as nothing we can either assert or lose to pragmatic argument.

But even on the most sympathetic reading, a question remains about the nature of Rorty's position. The question is most often articulated in terms of whether Rorty's position is the pragmatism of Dewey, or of James, or of another institutionalized sort. And to the extent that Rorty's position is something different, another question arises about whether it is even a *position*. Some think Rorty has only turned his back on philosophy, preferring to criticize the tradition from the safety of something like literary criticism. To be taken seriously, Rorty must be more than a critic of traditional philosophy whose criticism is unique to him and his particular time. Philosophers seem to want to ignore Rorty unless they can either read him as a relativist or think that someone *else* can do what he does. This is, in effect, to ask whether Rorty's philosophizing is *in* a *genre* or if it *is* a new *genre*. If the answer is neither, then Rorty will be at best a challenging gadfly.

INTELLIGIBILITY

The standard philosophical response to Rorty's critique is basically an epistemological one. It questions how what he claims to be the case is known, and known to be true. The underlying point of the response is to show that we cannot avoid issues of truth. The reply to antifoundationalist and anticorrespondist contentions is, in essence, to ask after the foundations and the truth of those contentions. This reply illustrates in a pointed way how the question arises about what philosophers are to do in a postphilosophical age, for doing philosophy seems to begin with questioning truth and foundations.

The standard response to Rorty cannot be dismissed too readily as a *petitio*, at least not until there is a positive answer to a different question, namely, whether Rorty's characterizations of correspondism and foundationalism are exhaustive. Rorty's is a critique of philosophy only if he has characterized philosophy properly. But Davidson offers what looks like a viable *philosophical* alternative to correspondism; and Williams seems to offer a viable *philosophical* way to understand objectivity in science. Unless Rorty's characterizations are exhaustive, his critique can be partially effective at best. We may find, as many contend, that all Rorty jettisons is what has already been abandoned: empiricist foundationalism and a simplistic correspondism.

The philosopher's concern with and reliance on truth and foundations can be described, in a very general sense, as testing for *intelligibility*. Much of what has passed for philosophy, at least since Aristotle's critique of Plato, has been assessment of intelligibility. Whether we are dealing with ideas or claims about the nature of ultimate reality, God, the soul, language, mind, or knowledge, critical philosophical work is mainly testing whether those ideas or claims are coherent, and hence possible.

Philosophical contentions of a positive sort have been contentions about the intelligibility of certain construals—God as necessary, the mind as matter-in-motion, language as replication; and negative claims have as inevitably been charges that given construals are unintelligible—mental acts as behavior, action as determined, sensa as the objects of knowledge. This becomes obvious when one considers that the tradition has precisely distinguished philosophical contentions from empirical ones as not verifiable, and hence the *only* test applicable to them is intelligibility.

But supposedly we are not speaking here of "surface" intelligibility, or the currency that even a bizarre notion may gain in common talk, and which Rorty is taken as endorsing when he rejects correspondism. At least the tradition would have us believe that we are speaking of something special that is supposedly congruent with some part of the structure of rationality. The importance of intelligibility to philosophical thought is underlain not only by the assumption that if something is intelligible, then it is capable of being true. The deeper assumption is that we are possessed of a rationality that is not only *our* reason but is universal, and that anything judged *un*intelligible is therefore something impossible, rather than just incomprehensible to us.

Reliance on intelligibility and unintelligibility was and is standard operating procedure for philosophical argumentation. For instance, Leibniz argued that an infinite series of causes was unintelligible and imposed intelligibility as the crucial criterion in his Sufficient Reason argument. The Logical Positivists thought they had discovered the ultimate philosophical device for determining intelligibility when they articulated their Verification Principle. The rejection of something as meaningless if neither analytic nor empirical—if confirmable neither by meaning nor by experience—appeared to be the final test for intelligibility. Philosophy could then leave it to the logicians or the scientists to test the actual truth or falsity of what was judged meaningful. In this way Logical Positivism embodied what Rorty is most concerned to defeat: the elevation of philosophy to the status of adjudicator of reason. To be the adjudicator of reason is to be the judge of intelligibility, and so of possibility. That is how traditional philosophers, especially epistemologists, conceive their role. Intelligibility is the prerequisite for truth. What this amounts to is an imposition of human rationality on reality. It is an interesting distortion of Protagoras's slogan, for "man is the measure" not because our beliefs and interests determine our world but because our mode of thought determines what can be.

The relevance of this discussion of intelligibility, aside from its importance to Rorty's critique, is that the thinking in question is applied to Rorty's position: his critique is often seen as based on an ultimately unintelligible nonrelativistic relativism, a nonphilosophical philosophical position. The trouble is that we do not understand how to dismiss correspondence and epistemological foundations without the dismissal amounting to relativism. Nor do we understand how philosophy can be over, given that we want to raise philosophical objections to the abandonment of all forms of correspondence and foundationalism. Rorty wants us to accept that discourses are "closed," that they have no external dimension analogous to that of scientific discourse, which is taken to include accurate representation. But it seems that discourses, if closed and free of external constraint—while perhaps internally consistent—cease to be *discourses* because they stop being *about* anything. This is Caputo's charge that Rorty leaves us with "just talk." As a consequence, it is difficult to maintain that Rorty is not a relativist.

Consider the following two cases: in the first, someone does something disallowed by cultural practice and is told, "That isn't done here"; in the second, someone says something disallowed by linguistic practice and is told, "We don't understand that." The former case may involve table manners, while the latter may concern something like Alfred North Whitehead's claim that "actual entities" are self-created. Rorty wants us to appreciate that nothing is added, in the second instance, by saying further: "That is unintelligible." And he wants us to appreciate that "We don't understand that" means "That is unintelligible" only in an innocuous sense, in that saying "That is unintelligible" says *no more* than "We don't understand that." But Rorty goes still further when he asks us to appreciate that "We don't understand that" does not differ in *kind* from "That isn't done here." His point is not only that there is nothing more to say when we disclaim understanding, that we do not thereby appeal to an *a priori* structure that is the ultimate standard of intelligibility. He also says that to disclaim understanding is no more—but no less—than to reject something as not allowed in a language game, as not part of our practice.

The immediate objection will be that some things simply cannot be allowed, regardless of practice, such as claims to having squared the circle or descriptions of the world as flat. With respect to the former, logical definition and implication are not at issue—not because securely *a priori* but because definitional—and these carry with them defined contexts that support the exclusions in question. It is the latter sort of remark that causes Rorty the most trouble. On one hand he wants to say the world is as it is, regardless of what we say or believe; on the other he wants productivity to be the sole criterion in the assessment of discourses or practices—and so deny assessment and constraint in terms of true description. The traditional philosopher, particularly the traditional epistemologist, sees that as making consensus the sole criterion for acceptability, and, unlike Rorty, will regard such consensus as forever contrastable with what is or might really be the case. Moreover, the traditionalist's retention of the conceptual/empirical distinction means that the problem of possible variance between consensus and truth—the variance Rorty disallows—might go on indefinitely, through chance success and conceptual adjustments at crucial junctures. However Rorty may try to undermine the enabling conditions for the charge of relativism, to abandon descriptive truth and extradiscursive justificatory criteria seems to cut individual discourses and intellectual epochs free of any common restraint. And this is all the more evident when we consider the premium Rorty puts on novelty in intellectual pursuits and the initiation of new discourses.

The appeal to intelligibility as the criterion for assessment of contentions and positions is the clearest expression of the philosophical tradition's conception of philosophy as the adjudicator of reason—and of what Rorty most wants to extirpate. Given'that appeal, it is charged that Rorty's version of pragmatism seems to fail the test of intelligibility because the traditional philosopher does not understand how Rorty's can be a position at all, much less a philosophical position, if he both denies relativism and establishes discourses as autonomous. Discourses are admittedly comparable in terms of productivity, but the comparison—like history—consists of stories in one discourse or vocabulary about other discourses or vocabularies. This point is obvious when Rorty denies that the history of science manifests real progress in inquiry.

The specific question of Rorty's reading of Dewey, and, by implication, the general question of how we can construe Rorty's views, were raised and discussed in a symposium on *Consequences* that tried to determine what kind of pragmatist Rorty is.[4] In the symposium Rorty is criticized for his interpretation of Dewey, especially his efforts to detach and dismiss Dewey's concern with methodology as something beyond the practices of a given language community. Rorty is accused of disallowing the methodology, which Dewey strove so hard to develop, in order to shape Dewey's thought to his own antifoundationalism. Dewey's commitment to the progressiveness of inquiry is too close to foundationalism for Rorty's taste. This alleged distortion of Dewey is interpreted as a consequence of a questionable appropriation of pragmatism, one which focuses exclusively on the rejection of correspondence, essentialism, and foundationalism—while eschewing the realism, optimistic conceptions of science and methodology, and tolerance of natural kinds that characterize much of classical pragmatism. In effect summarizing his own and his cosymposiast's views, Abraham Edel remarks that in Rorty "there is no pragmatic philosophy, only a pragmatic overcoming of Philosophy."[5]

Edel goes on to charge that Rorty

> has softened the notion of knowledge more than is required to see the continuities of science, philosophy, and poetry, and that pragmatism not only admits of but actually employs . . . a view of the growth of knowledge *and its impact on philosophical ideas* which enable us to judge better and worse in philosophy.[6]

To develop a contrast to Rorty, Edel portrays Dewey as a pragmatist who recognizes progress in inquiry or the growth of knowledge. The implication is that to *be* a pragmatist one need not go as far as Rorty has, and that by going as far as he does go he makes his position untenable.

The issue between Edel and R. W. Sleeper on the one hand, and Rorty on the other, is seen by Edel and Sleeper as whether Dewey was the edifying revolutionary Rorty pictures, one whose views are therefore available to Rorty as a model of postphilosophical thinking, or whether Dewey was a more evolutionary thinker. The force of the latter conclusion would not suffice to defeat Rorty, but it would put the onus entirely on him to clarify what sort of pragmatism he offers. Both Edel and Sleeper stress Dewey's methodological and metaphysical concerns and projects, especially his commitment to Peirce's notion that inquiry is progressive. In this way they place both Dewey and pragmatism within the philosophical tradition, while insisting on its critical nature. They also suggest, incidentally, that James's version of pragmatism is closer to Rorty's conception than is Dewey's. But beyond interpretive and exegetical issues, Edel and Sleeper see Rorty's alleged distortion of Dewey as manifesting the general philosophical unviability of his views. Edel contends that

> As long as we can think of knowledge and its growth, and the possibility of judgments of better and worse in respect to it, however

analyzed, we can retain a notion of the mainstream of philosophical problems.[7]

Sleeper remarks on Rorty's apparent indifference to Dewey's conception of the productivity of inquiry: "Like Dewey, Rorty *does* see 'meanings' as 'means', but he treats them as 'ungrounded' and not—as Dewey taught us to see them—as . . . *emergent* from inquiry."[8] It is the *growth* of knowledge that Rorty precludes. Therefore, no history or retrospective view can support "judgments of better or worse" regarding discourses or vocabularies. Any such views will only be stories about earlier stories—whether in new, or the same, vocabularies.

Rorty sees the issue between himself and Edel and Sleeper as whether or not a certain construal of Dewey's views is productive. With respect to Dewey and pragmatism, Rorty tells us that, while Edel is largely right about how Dewey saw his own project,

> a thinker's own self-image may not be usable by his heirs. . . . So whereas Edel thinks of me as "taking pragmatism out of the mainstream of philosophy" because I neglect "the role of growing knowledge and its impact on philosophical ideas", I . . . am trying to adapt pragmatism to a changed intellectual environment by emphasizing the differences rather than the similarities with the philosophical tradition.[9]

Rorty's concern is less with getting Dewey *right*—in terms of the sort of historical understanding recognized as possible by Jones—than with whether Dewey can be useful to us in our present situation.[10] For Rorty, interpretation of Dewey is just that—interpretation. Whether or not to allow interpretation beyond Dewey's own intentions raises for Rorty the issue of whether or not philosophizing is to be hermeneutical and pragmatic. Rorty's response to Edel and Sleeper is surprising only in one respect. He not only distances himself from his earlier confident interpretation of Dewey, he also admits that perhaps using the term "pragmatism" was ill-advised. In his disclaimers he tries to acknowledge his own lack of originality by attributing a number of views to Dewey and pragmatism.[11] But he does not argue that Dewey was mistaken about his own project, or that Edel and Sleeper have misinterpreted Dewey. Instead he defends the productivity of emphasizing some things in Dewey while de-emphasizing the metaphysical, methodological, and foundational aspects of his work. We are told that "the whole idea of 'analysis of methods' is misconceived, and thus . . . 'logic', conceived as Dewey conceived of it, is a subject not worth developing."[12] Rorty aims not to *re*interpret Dewey, but to ignore much of what Dewey prized in order to avail ourselves of what is of value to us in Dewey's work. To see the rightness of this, "All that is needed is the realization that we shall never have a language, either scientific or philosophical, which does not make reference to the situation we are in at the moment."[13] So it is hopeless to pursue Dewey's interest in determining how inquiry achieves an extradiscursive dimension.

But Rorty is cognizant of the dangers of idealist implications and of being seen as "weakening" knowledge:

> The idea that brilliant scientific innovators reshape the object rather than merely predicating different attributes of it is a theme common to Dewey and Kuhn, but the problem for both has been to put this idea in a non-idealistic way, one which admits that the objects are there before mind comes along, and remain what they were while being known. I think that analytic philosophy gave us a vocabulary which enabled us to avoid the idealistic flavor . . . by permitting us to say: Aristotle and Galileo and Darwin were presented with exactly the same objects, but there is no *neutral* epistemological language which permits us to say what those objects were.[14]

Rorty's point here is clear and persuasive: without falling into idealism, we can say what we need to say about objectivity being unachievable because neutral language is impossible. What is less clear is the matter of the growth of knowledge. His response to Edel is decidedly weak. Essentially, Rorty again queries the role of the epistemologists once the hope of a fundamental methodology is abandoned. But the *actual* growth of knowledge will not go away, according to both Edel and Williams. Rorty's only reply seems to be that the growth or progress which Williams and Edel and others think so obvious is only the particular construal of history from our present standpoint. This view maintains that what we perceive as the growth of knowledge—and the consequent influence of that growth on philosophical ideas—is not independent of our present beliefs and discourses. It is not *real* in the way that at least some of its objects are real.

A new shift out of "normal" science into a period of crisis would supposedly sweep away that putative growth or progress. But the strength of
Williams's and Edel's objection—and the point of my retrospective
objectivity—is that when we look back over the history of science, if not
history generally, we think we see that previous shifts out of normal
science have somehow been cumulative. For instance, the shift from the
physics of Newton to that of Heisenberg appears to have been an advance
on the shift from the physics of Aristotle to that of Galileo. Of course Rorty
will argue that precisely that perception of advance constitutes a crucial
part of our present construal of the history of science, and that nothing
beyond that construal constitutes such an advance.

Kai Nielsen has pursued Williams's charge in his "Scientism, Pragmatism and the Fate of Philosophy." Nielsen endorses most of Williams's
criticisms, and adds that while

> There indeed is no such thing as nature's own language or a vocabul-
> ary in which the world demands to be described . . . . [T]hat by itself
> is not enough to make it . . . senseless or even mistaken to speak
> of . . . an independent world that we try to describe with varying
> degrees of success. Pragmatists . . . realized that there was something
> special about science . . . . Rorty in a very unpragmatist manner
> seems to think that there is nothing special . . . about science.
>
> . . . [E]ven if we cannot say anything very useful about scientific
> method, we might, as Popper believes we can, be able to say some-
> thing non-mythological about the objective progress of science in
> finding out what the world is like.[15]

And Nielsen adds, "Indeed scientific theory is cumulative in that it . . .
can explain why some of the predictions of previous theories were true and
others false."[16] Nielsen is most in agreement here with Williams's point
that science can explain how creatures like us understand the world as we
do. Nielsen makes two points, one about science as such, and one about
pragmatists. The latter is that Dewey and Peirce, as well as later pragmatists like Sidney Hook and Ernest Nagel, and contemporary pragmatists like Sidney Morgenbesser, all saw science and scientific method as
having a special place, as providing real progress that differentiated them
from other discourses. Nielsen is concerned to endorse Rorty's rejection of
empiricist foundationalism while preserving some methodological objec-

tivism for science, especially social science. But the burden of the foregoing is that, unless we are willing to dismiss pragmatists from Dewey to Morgenbesser as inconsistent and self-deceived, pragmatism does not preclude a modified methodological objectivity or recognition of truth in something like Davidson's sense: that is, that at least a large part of what we believe and say "corresponds" to the world, as evidenced by our progress in inquiry.

To make some headway we might summarize the preceding as follows: Rorty wants us to accept that our bases for action are always our own. By this I mean he rejects the idea that any basis for action can be provided *a priori* by recourse to anything beyond our beliefs and practices. Nor can satisfaction of *a priori* standards show anything to be a suitable or better basis for action. This is the heart of Rorty's pragmatism: there is nothing to either guarantee or preclude the productivity of a course of action, discourse, or single proposition. At most we can judge discourses, propositions, and actions as conforming or not to past and present practices, and as productive or not in light of past or present objectives and developments.

There can of course be *more* of whatever we count as knowledge, but it cannot be cumulative in the sense that it bulks large enough to transcend, and so unite, our historically individual beliefs, language games, and practices, or to justify our methodologies. Knowledge cannot grow to the proportions of an ahistorical or extracultural watershed of understanding, for nothing can *be* knowledge if it is not deemed so within a particular language game or practice. Rorty, then, must downplay Dewey's efforts to achieve a methodology for the *production* of knowledge. He insists that all the stories that serve us as bases for action are equal to one another prior to demonstrating themselves successful or otherwise. And he further insists that when a story does demonstrate itself a productive basis for action, it does not thereby reveal something *further*, for example, that it is a better description of how things really are.

But this is where we run into trouble, as we saw with Williams's critique, for in science we have a set of related stories that provide very reliable bases for action—bases so reliable that we feel they must share some special trait, such as true descriptiveness. And we think that science manifests precisely the real progressiveness that Rorty rejects, and that Dewey and Peirce expected of properly conceived and conducted inquiry.

A FIRST SUMMATION

The main issue in this chapter is whether we can make real progress in inquiry, and part of that question concerns whether continuing to do philosophy—like Davidson's efforts to defeat skepticism and my efforts here—is something we must do *in spite* of Rorty. I do not think Rorty's work constitutes a *new way* of philosophizing, or a new *genre* in which we might participate, so the alternative is not doing philosophy his way. If Rorty offers something new, over and above his critique of the tradition, it is a wholly historicist *perspective*, as opposed to a position. What so many condemn as his lack of a clear positive position is simply his unwillingness to offer one in his role as critic. Rorty seems to think that the critic, evaluating a concert and finding fault with the performance and conception of the work, does not presume to take the baton and conduct it himself. If Rorty's work is edifying, it is in virtue of the scope of his critique: the order of magnitude of the enterprise he finds fault with. Rorty does not offer us an alternative philosophical methodology. But now our question is this: If the charges against Rorty, of idealism or some form of nonrealism, can at least be seriously debated, as indicated in my treatment of Meynell, then is Rorty's critical position—even if unique—a viable one? Is philosophy over? Or is Rorty's position vitiated by the "discourse egalitarianism" evident in his denial of real progress in inquiry? Or is there a third option, namely, that a certain sort of philosophy *is* over and that Rorty is therefore partly right in spite of being wrong about progress in inquiry?

As a proposed new perspective on inquiry and all our other intellectual activities, Rorty's viewpoint may be wanting because it distorts or denies a crucial aspect of at least one central intellectual activity. He denies not only the crucial nature of scientific objectivity and scientific progress, but also the centrality we assign to our present scientific interpretation of inquiry. Inquiry is not governed, even passively, by its objects, so our use of science as a paradigm of inquiry is doubly wrong: There is nothing special about scientific methodology, and any progress in inquiry we might congratulate ourselves on will always be *internal* to our discourses and practices:

> Let me sum up by offering a . . . final characterization of pragmatism: it is the doctrine that there are no constraints on inquiry save conversational ones—no wholesale constraints derived from the na-

ture of the objects, or of the mind, or of language, but only those . . . constraints provided by the remarks of our fellow inquirers.[17]

Rorty thinks he is only reminding us that, however vehemently we assert certain propositions, and however staunchly we defend certain procedures, we change our minds. We stop talking about phlogiston or monads, and we forget about casting runes or exorcism, no matter how important such talk and practice might have been at a given time, or how certain we might have been that without such talk and practice the world could not be engaged or described. Quite simply, many feel that we have come too far for that sort of upheaval to occur again, that inquiry has been too successful for its edifice to be vacated in favor of another or for it to crumble of its own weight. Even Kuhnian paradigm shifts seem to occur *within* something that we deem "science" in a very broad, but still meaningful, sense.

Descartes sought to initiate a discourse and a methodology constrained by necessity that would *never* be abandoned or radically changed, and thus initiated modern epistemology. History stresses Descartes's fascination with the progress of science and cites enthusiasm for similar progress in philosophy as his motivation. He is pictured as a revolutionary. But that view is anachronistic. Descartes *was* impressed by intellectual revolution, but his project was ultraconservative: to prevent a recurrence of such a revolution, to insure that human knowledge would never again be shaken as it was in his time. Against this, Rorty wants us to live in constant anticipation of change, in perennial distrust of our convictions and practices, and appreciative of the enrichment of culture that follows on multiplicity of views and change.

We resist, convinced that there has been too much success in judging some bases for action better than others, and that that success is cumulative— and further convinced that the reasons for success cannot lie totally within our attitudes and beliefs, our construals and practices. Some stories must be *inherently* better bases for action because they "get something right." Rorty does not deny that some stories serve us better, but he balks at the "inherently" and refuses to allow that there is anything underlying success—or any way we might insure, prior to acting, that a story will be productive.

Rorty accepts what Dewey may have avoided: the realization that to reject truth as any sort of correspondence is to preclude granting a privileged status of greater inherent reliability to any discourse. *A priori* reliability can only be perceived in terms of some conformity of the structure of descriptive and practical techniques to *how things are*. Repeated evidence of reliability does not suffice, for it can never preclude change. For Dewey, truth, or warranted assertibility, was essentially a coherence of judgments; that coherence was in turn the basis for action, and its proper test was consequential. A "false" judgment was one that did not cohere with a given productive set, and that failed to result in as much or more productivity when acted on. The contents of experience—in effect the world—were a coherence of events. The distinction between what is real and what is not real was one of coherence, or its lack, with the set of experiences/meanings/objects that constituted the most stable and productive bases for action. Dewey very likely had no business endorsing Peirce's methodological optimism, not after writing that "all natural events are subject to reconsideration and revision; they are readapted to meet the requirements of conversation."[18]

Dewey's commitment to the progressiveness of inquiry may be less clear than Edel or Sleeper think; but while Rorty does not make Dewey's putative mistake of aspiring to an ahistorical methodology in spite of rejecting everything that makes one seem necessary as well as apparently possible, Rorty's consistency costs him credibility. Dewey retains his place in the tradition more or less to the extent that he believed in the progressiveness of inquiry. He remains credible because his possible inconsistency is seen as a manifestation of his ongoing commitment to philosophical canons and objectives, and so Dewey is counted as a serious philosopher. Sleeper remarks that "Robert Frost used to complain about poets who wrote blank verse . . . [that it] was . . . like playing tennis with the net down. Rorty's pragmatism *is* like that . . . in a way Dewey's . . . is not."[19]

What we have is this: Rorty does not offer a new way of doing philosophy; instead he says philosophy is over. The position from which he says that is a putative pragmatism, but one free of even the problematic commitment to progress in inquiry. Rorty's position may be vitiated by his denial of real growth in knowledge. Consistent with his views, he is "playing with the net down," contending against philosophical methodology without regard for its canons—charging that those canons are based on unproductive notions such as that of correspondence. Unlike poets using blank verse, who have other options, the enlightened pragmatist understands there is no alternative to conversation, and the drift of the conversation is that we no longer want to talk about truth and foundations. But many find this too dubious a basis for the claim that philosophy is over—especially since the charge that Rorty is arguing without constraint seems itself a paradigmatic philosophical objection. More specifically, his denial of progress in science or inquiry seems unacceptable because of a possibly distorted or ignorant understanding of science and scientific procedure—an understanding, furthermore, that can be argumentatively *made out* as distorted or ignorant, and hence as one which is not the basis for a preferable conversation.

Rorty's claim that philosophy is over is consistent with his denial of progress in inquiry, for both are part of his contention that our discourses—especially the philosophical—are just ways of coping. So if Rorty is wrong about progress or objectivity in science, he may well be wrong about at least some aspects of philosophy. It seems clear, for one thing, that the defense of progress in inquiry conducted by Williams is a *philosophical* one, so its effectiveness is evidence of the viability of philosophical methodology. The conclusion, then, is that as long as there are viable philosophical critiques of Rorty's critique, philosophy continues to be more than conversation.

But Rorty will construe criticism as itself so much more conversation. Rorty's rejoinder must be that Williams's or my objections to his views are themselves attempts at conversational restraint. For instance, he will say that any progress established by Williams's arguments is still contained by a delineable discourse, the scientific, and therefore open to change or abandonment with that discourse. Rorty's rejection of the objectivism necessary to give contrast to the relativism he is charged with is in fact a refusal to take part in the philosophical conversation, a refusal to be bound by its rules. But the complication is that he does not only want to withdraw; he wants *us* to abandon the philosophical conversation because it is not a productive one, and because it incorporates ideas that our present vocabularies and discourses do not tolerate.

It does seem, then, that Rorty has no position as such, that he is only using pragmatism in an eclectic manner to overcome philosophy. Sleeper lists the differences between Rorty and other pragmatists, contending that

> On the face of it, Rorty's pragmatism seems hardly to qualify. Unlike Peirce, Rorty has nothing to do with "realism" . . . . Unlike James, Rorty has no use for psychology . . . . Unlike Schiller, Rorty wants a "Pragmatism Without Method" . . . *unlike* Mead he does not see his theory of meaning in metaphysical perspective, the perspective that Charles W. Morris called "emergent realism" and to which Dewey

subscribed—or acquiesced in 1932 . . . . Unlike *both* Dewey and
Quine, Rorty eschews all ontological commitments . . . . Rorty admits no "natural kinds".[20]

Sleeper admits that Rorty is a pragmatist in his rejection of correspondism
and essentialism, but he laments how "pragmatism" has lost its useful-
ness and how Rorty has neglected the positive contributions of the
philosophy he rejects. It is true that "pragmatism" seems overused when
applied to the views of James and Quine, Peirce *and* Rorty. But if we put
aside the doctrinal question, and ask about the spirit of Rorty's views, we
may better understand how his is a position. Speaking of how the
"thinking process does not go on endlessly . . . but seeks outlet through
reference to particular experiences," Dewey articulates the pragmatism
Rorty so admires in this way:

> [The thinking process] . . . is tested . . . not, however, as if a theory
> could be tested by directly comparing it with facts—an obvious
> impossibility—but through use in facilitating commerce with facts. It
> is tested as glasses are tested; things are looked at through the
> medium of specific meanings to see if thereby they assume a more
> orderly and clearer aspect, if they are less blurred and obscure.[21]

To capture what Rorty is saying, we need only add to Dewey's point that
we cannot look at the facts *without* glasses. Some glasses serve us better
than others, but we must employ one or another pair, we must look at the
world through one or another construal. And as long as we cannot
compare theories to facts, we cannot enshrine any theory or methodology
as inherently productive. The issue between Rorty and Williams is that
Williams thinks there is an *indirect* way of comparing the whole of science
to the facts, just as Davidson thinks we must understand how language
corresponds as a whole to the world. And here again we wonder about
Rorty's convenient indifference to history. As record-keepers we have
access to construals of the world different from our immediate ones.
Hermeneutical care is called for to make those construals real for us, but
we *can* consider them sufficiently to appreciate their strengths and weak-
nesses. This may not amount to awareness of stages in an inexorable
march toward the *best* construals, but surely it makes evident certain

emergent aspects of inquiry, such as science's internally generated objectivity.

But Rorty eschews that sort of thinking. There just *is* no way that our beliefs and sayings can ever amount to more than historically bounded construals. Rorty's pragmatic position or perspective draws a compelling conclusion about the nature of our intellectual enterprise—but not a conclusion to an *argument*:

> Pragmatists follow Hegel in saying that "philosophy is its time grasped in thought." Antipragmatists follow Plato in striving for an escape from conversation to something atemporal which lies in the background of all possible conversations. I do not think one can decide between Hegel and Plato save by meditating on the past efforts of the philosophical tradition to escape from time and history. One can see these efforts as . . . getting better . . . [or] as doomed and perverse. . . . [T]he decision has to be made by reading the history of philosophy and drawing a moral.[22]

Just so. But the moral Williams, Davidson, Nielsen, and I draw is that there is at least more to philosophical and scientific methodology than Rorty allows, and that our discourses, though ways of coping—where they can be delineated—are better or worse in virtue of how the world is, not in some absolute sense.

I have come to feel less and less satisfied with Rorty's position—which I hope to have dealt with sympathetically. But I find it very difficult to say something that will count against him. As indicated in chapters 3 and 4, there is no doubt that the issues of truth and progress in inquiry have not evaporated. However, their persistence now carries the taint of prejudicial construal, so their survival is by itself insufficient. The question is what to offer as additional support.

One noteworthy point is that Rorty's position turns on our being able to delineate "the philosophical conversation" and "the scientific discourse" from among others. I do not believe we can do that in the way Rorty requires. There is no longer *a* scientific discourse that we can move in and out of at will and contrast with the literary or the religious. The sort of progress or objectivity Williams defends now permeates all our "discourses." Whether knowingly or otherwise, this fact is actually what Rorty seeks to change in proposing that the literary shape our thought more. But the point here is that the metaphor-set, or vocabulary, of science is no longer isolated. It is integral to our practices in a way that is not displaceable by the literary or some other competing discourse. What is most important here is that, if we can no longer speak of "the scientific" discourse or vocabulary, it may be less because of its influence as a specific vocabulary than because our discourse and vocabularies cannot be delineated in a way that lets us describe our history as a series of changes among different and discontinuous vocabularies and discourses.

Does the question of the delineability of discourses or vocabularies prevent Rorty from drawing the moral he wants to draw from a consideration of the history of science or philosophy? His main defense against the claim that history exhibits real progress is that scientific, philosophical, or any other history is just a story in one vocabulary or discourse about another—usually earlier—vocabulary or discourse. But if vocabularies and discourses are not delineable—at least not as distinct as Rorty implies—then Rorty's position looks very dubious. If there is no significant plurality of discourses and vocabularies, then the one we have is probably not accidental, and assumes its identity because of true descriptive content. Without a plurality of metaphor-sets, or something similar, the very commonness of something recognized as a *single* vocabulary or discourse, albeit with internal variations, is evidence that it is grounded in something other than practice. If shifts such as occurred between Aristotle and Newton, and between Newton and Einstein, are more continuous than Rorty suggests; if there is no worrying problem of translatability, as Davidson argues there is not; then there is reason to think that our vocabulary or discourse is less of our making than dictated by how things are.

Rorty thinks that the intellectual enterprise is the study and history of metaphor; that scientific revolutions are wholesale metaphor-shifts; and that "progress" means doing something new, or taking up the new and forgetting the old. But, oddly enough, the way Rorty breaks up the continuity of old and new metaphor-sets—a continuity that supports the growth of knowledge—looks too much like making them alternative conceptual schemes. Rorty thinks he avoids that embarrassing consequence because he has rejected the scheme/content distinction. But his avowals may not be enough if we feel he has in fact reintroduced just the distinction Davidson denied. On the other hand, if we read Rorty sympathetically, and do not make too much of the differences among discourses or metaphors, how is he to *preclude* the cumulative growth of knowledge? Putting the point differently, how can he conclusively restrict us to time and history? How can he disallow that our intellectual enterprise might achieve an external dimension in the sense of acquiring real descriptive content?

My feeling is that Rorty would dismiss the foregoing by admitting that we *do* capture how things are in our growing competence at coping with the world. I think that he would see that concession as harmless, and insist only that we cannot *prove* anything, and that we certainly cannot develop a failsafe methodology on that basis. But that brings us back to the point that he is really rejecting what has long been discarded, namely, the achievement of Cartesian certainty. If the burden of the charge that philosophy is over is that *Cartesian* philosophy is over, we must agree—but we must also judge that contention less than original.

Still, we are left unsatisfied; we think we may be missing something. I hope in the next, and final, chapter to say something more definitive about Rorty's pragmatism and about pragmatism generally. In particular, I shall pursue the questions of how philosophy might be over, in spite of Davidson and Williams and my own project, and of what we might say about progress in inquiry. I shall also say more about how our "discourses" are not as delineable as Rorty thinks.

Notes

1. Taylor, "Minerva."
2. It is of significance that Tarski does not accept this view that is so often attached to his semantic theory of truth. Consider the following passage, brought to my attention by my colleague E. J. Bond:

> ... I was by no means surprised to learn (in a discussion devoted to these problems) that in a group of people who were questioned only 15% agreed that *"true"* means for them *"agreeing with reality"*, while 90% agreed that a sentence such as *"it is snowing"* is true if, and only if, it is snowing. [Presumably 5% agreed to both.] (Alfred Tarski, "The Semantic Conception of Truth and the Foundations of Semantics," in Herbert Feigl and Wilfrid Sellars, *Readings in Philosophical Analysis* [New York: Appleton-Century-Crofts, 1949], 70)

3. See Rorty, *Mirror*, part 3.
4. See John J. McDermott, R. W. Sleeper, Abraham Edel, and Richard Rorty, "Symposium on Rorty's *Consequences of Pragmatism*," *Transactions of the Charles S. Peirce Society* 21 (1985): 1–48.

5. Ibid., 22.
6. Ibid.
7. Ibid., 30–31.
8. Ibid., 11.
9. Ibid., 47.
10. Speaking of traditional philosophy as capital-P Philosophy, and of the pragmatism he endorses as lowercase philosophy, Rorty says:

> . . . the first tradition thinks of truth as a vertical relationship between
> representations and what is represented. The second tradition thinks of
> truth horizontally—as the culminating reinterpretation of our predecessors'
> reinterpretation of their predecessors' reinterpretation. (*Consequences*, xlii)

11. McDermott and others, "Symposium," 39–40.
12. Ibid., 41.
13. Ibid., 43.
14. Ibid., 42.
15. Nielsen, "Scientism," 34–35. For a related critique, see Alisdair MacIntyre,
"Philosophy, the 'Other' Disciplines, and Their Histories: A Rejoinder to
Richard Rorty," *Soundings* 65: 127–145.
16. Nielsen, "Scientism," 36.
17. Rorty, *Consequences*, 165.
18. John Dewey, *Experience and Nature*, repub. of 2d ed. (New York: Dover, 1958),
166.
19. McDermott and others, "Symposium," 14.
20. Ibid., 11.
21. John Dewey, *Essays in Experimental Logic* (Chicago: University of Chicago,
1916; reprint New York: Dover, 1966), 198.
22. Rorty, *Consequences*, 174.

Chapter 6

The Limits of Pragmatism

PRELIMINARY REMARKS

It has not been my intention to survey Rorty's views in an extended way. For one thing, he is a prolific writer whose works vary in tone, in focus, and often in emphasis and orientation. A comprehensive character-ization and assessment would have necessitated a work considerably longer than the present one. Moreover, Rorty's books and essays are remarkably rich in implications, allusions, and learning. Not enough time has elapsed for adequate critical interaction with the texts. We still hear mainly Rorty's voice; his interpretation of the texts still dominates. At the outset I said that enough time had passed to consider what is *central* to Rorty's pragmatism. I suspect it will be some years before we see a definitive work on the full range of Rorty's writings—and even longer if he produces his promised book on Heidegger.

In this chapter I attempt to do justice to the "therapeutic" aspect of Rorty's critique and to articulate more perspicuously how I think that critique is limited. I also want to demonstrate how the limitations of Rorty's critique are limitations of pragmatism generally. In the latter endeavor my interpretation of pragmatism is closer to Dewey and Peirce than to James or Rorty. In a word, my assessment of Rorty's critique is that it has focused our contemporary fallibilism and historicism, added depth to both, but led Rorty to unsupportable conclusions—extreme historicist conclusions that are neither integral to classical pragmatism nor necessary to a viable modern pragmatism. Rorty is reminiscent of early Greek skeptics who took their own arguments too much to heart. Rorty is right, but only to a point. A sort of philosophy *is* over, and certain of our hopes and projects must be abandoned as unproductive. But I think he is wrong in trying to *preclude* a special kind of assessment of our history and knowledge—in other words, he is wrong to think that his critique of our old conception of philosophy and its various distinctions renders vacuous the distinction between intra- and extradiscourse knowledge, thereby making claims to well-grounded historical knowledge impossible. This move on Rorty's part is too much like the rejection by post-Cartesians of the mind/body distinction in favor of one or another side of it. Somehow Rorty's rejection of the distinction between intra- and extradiscourse knowledge becomes an affirmation of the exhaustiveness of intradiscourse knowledge.

My main point is that Rorty's lesson—that there is no distinction between knowledge internal to some discourse or perspective and "objective" knowledge external to all perspectives and discourses—is a lesson worth learning. Nonetheless, learning that lesson should not require us to accept the problematic idea that none of our knowledge can provide us with grounds for conclusions that overreach limited sets of discourses. Rorty might grant most of this, but the difference between us is that he wants to conceive of such overreaching knowledge as so many "metanarratives," discourses about discourses or stories about stories, which differ from their object-narratives—in effect intradiscourse knowledge—only in breadth. I want some knowledge to differ in what I can only call authority; and what I mean by "authority" is that productivity and reliability in such metanarratives, at least in the case of science, is a function of *correctness*.

Rorty, rather like John Locke, has tried to counter Cartesian *a priorism* with "historical, plain method."[1] The rejection of correspondism and foundationalism is, above all, a counter to *a priorism* in its broad sense of anything that might yield nonperspectival, ahistorical knowledge. The main message is that there is no way to describe ourselves, our thoughts, our language, our practices, or the world, *neutrally*: in "nature's own"—or "reason's own"—vocabulary. As for philosophy, the way it is over—and how that is evident once we acknowledge the impossibility of neutral description—is that philosophical contentions about reason, knowledge, and truth are never more than epochal pronouncements, as limited to time and history as hemlines or necktie widths. Rorty proffers a reading of the history and invites us to draw a conclusion: that the traditional philosophical enterprise has failed; that its central notions, such as correspondence, are unworkable; and that we have not the slightest reason to believe or hope that we ever did or ever might escape from time and history. In the process history becomes a fundamentally disjointed series of narratives and metanarratives—a series that is continuous only in the sense that the subject matter of each subsequent narrative is almost always an earlier narrative or set of narratives. Occasionally, when a particular century is fortunate enough to have one or another edifying thinker, wholly novel narratives or discourses are initiated.[2] But inclusion of earlier narratives in a given narrative does not make for cumulative progress, for the current narrative is always one of a huge number of possible ones, each with different emphases and construals and none with grounds better than the others, whether the narrative in question is literary, historical, or scientific.

The burden of what I have said in the foregoing chapters is that, with respect to *some* understanding of truth-as-correspondence (in the sense of the world determining what is true), and with respect to retrospective, emergent evidence of cumulative growth in knowledge, some of our beliefs and some threads in our history assume proportions beyond the epochal. Though there are ambitious projects directed against Rortyan historicism, such as Nielsen's attempt to elaborate a Habermasian critical theory that offers some of the scope and necessity promised by traditional epistemology, Davidson and Williams supply enough reason to think that the intellectual enterprise is not as perspectively fragmented as Rorty thinks, that it is not a sequence of discontinuous discourses and stories about discourses, and hence that it may now exhibit real progress.[3] As suggested in the last chapter, I find problematic the distinctness of discourses that Rorty needs and assumes to prevent anything approaching cumulative, interepochal growth in knowledge. If discourses, vocabularies, or metaphor-sets can be considered essentially continuous or hierarchically integrated despite Rorty's critique, then perhaps we can make out how *enough* history and *enough* inquiry let us, if not escape time and history, at least assess history in a way that goes beyond the mere telling of new stories.

But Rorty's perhaps excessive historicism should not jeopardize the beneficial force of his critique. Rorty's argument should make philosophers more conscious of the need for the Socratic virtues in discussion, dispel methodological complacency, and bring down the arrogance of false professionalism. Rorty should successfully make the points he tries to make in such articles as "The World Well Lost" and "Philosophy in America Today."[4] Unfortunately, the philosophical establishment's response to his criticism has been conservative and defensive. Perhaps the most common attitude is that Rorty's critique and dismissal of philosophy manifests either that he is failing to conform to still reliable philosophical standards or that he is conforming to them while disingenuously rejecting them.[5] And while few defend foundationalism in its classical empiricist form, many buttress the charges of indifference to standards and disingenuousness with appeal to an apparently innocuous form of foundationalism, by talking of "obvious" truths about cups being on tables or torture being bad.[6]

The charge in question seems too simple, and, as we have seen, Rorty is very concerned to show how at least the first half begs the question against his contentions. Nonetheless, the appeal to obvious truths has this much in its favor: We simply do not understand how being right about certain things is a matter of what our fellows will allow, not a matter of truth. But we should distrust this lack of understanding as possibly prejudiced, as perhaps a blindness due to the momentum of our practices. But even if we feel that distrust, it is more difficult to doubt the general cumulative growth of knowledge in science. Regretfully, rather than respond positively by examining how structured and cooperative inquiry with a detailed history may yield some measure of objectivity, many respond negatively by characterizing Rorty as running roughshod over philosophical canons that he has not adequately impugned. The latter attitude prevents productive, synthesizing discussion by reducing the defense of philosophy to the reiteration of the traditional view, and thereby circumscribing both the tradition and Rorty's views as intractably opposed positions. The strongest impression I have from discussing Rorty with professional philosophers is that his pragmatism, which is mainly an *attitude* toward thought and inquiry, will be circumscribed, and its power limited, by being construed as a competing philosophical thesis. There will be debate about Rorty's relation to, and interpretation of, James and Dewey; the issue of idealistic implications in his pragmatism will be considered; and the lack of positive proposals on various topics will be deplored at length. Rorty's position will gain adherents, but *as* a position. In short, the critic who left the ivory tower to undermine its foundations will be reinstalled in the tower.

There are practical constraints on philosophers, as well as doctrinal and ideological ones. Few academic philosophers can follow the professionally suicidal admonition to abandon their discipline in favor of conversation. Rorty may be able to leave the Princeton philosophy department to go to the University of Virginia as a university professor of the humanities, but few others will have that sort of opportunity. Their only option, assuming serious interest in Rorty, will be to teach courses on him, write papers about his pragmatism, and so on. There is, of course, nothing wrong with that. It is viable academic activity; but it will limit how professional philosophers may be influenced by Rorty in particular and pragmatism in general. While philosophers should perhaps resist Rorty's call to abandon academic philosophy and usher in the postphilosophic era, they ought to be more receptive to his ideas and consider seriously how certain ways of philosophizing *are* over. However, they simply cannot afford that, in the broadest sense, for economic reasons. Their livelihoods and their considerable intellectual and methodological investments must be given priority. Consciously or otherwise, they must make Rorty a subject of *established* philosophical discourse, which is, in effect, to deny him the status of an external critic with significant influence. And there is something else, a more elusive factor that further blunts Rorty's influence on academic philosophers. *Teaching* Rorty is difficult. Students respond favorably, but superficially, to his critique. They consider it iconoclastic and exciting, but few of them have had the time to feel the grip of what he rejects. They may appreciate, in an abstract way, that it is unproductive to do epistemology, but few can feel *liberated* by Rorty's critique because they have not been captives of Bernstein's "Cartesian Anxiety." This means that, for thousands of working professional philosophers, Rorty's critique cannot be integrated into their day-to-day teaching.

Opposed to the conservative reaction of professional philosophers to Rorty's critique is the widespread, and sometimes facile, response of academics who are *not* philosophers, and who see Rorty's work as admirable, but pertinent only to the views and aspirations of professional philosophers. That is, they think Rorty is good for *us*, but not of great import for *them*. They tend to judge his critique as narrowly applicable to the pretentions of academic philosophy, because they think their own disciplines have abandoned those pretensions. Many social scientists, for instance, think that faith in an ahistorical methodology or in correspondism is simply naive. *They* do not need to be encouraged to abandon foundationalism or an algorithmic conception of science. And most literary critics wonder at the controversy, thinking that philosophers should have long ago stopped conceiving of language as capable of portraying reality and, even more astonishingly, of communicating those imagined portraits. The trouble, though, is that those who think Rorty's critique an internecine matter often fail to identify correspondist or foundationalist strains in their own thought and disciplines. The social scientist is prepared to listen to Jurgen Habermas, but may not hear Rorty's cautions about Habermas's latent foundationalism; the literary critic is prepared to listen to Jaques Derrida, but not to Rorty's suggestions about Derrida's limited value as a gadfly.[7]

Rorty, then, is something of a voice in the wilderness, and the therapeutic value of his critique may be lost. Those to whom his message is most directly addressed deflect it and blunt its point by forcing it into established categories. And those to whom it speaks more indirectly—and to whom Rorty implicitly appeals—regard that message as dated. It seems, then, that Rorty's "hard saying" that "there is nothing deep down inside us except what we have put there ourselves" is translated into either a problematic partisan contention or a truism.[8] But then Rorty is in good company. Nietzsche and Dewey failed to revamp philosophy—the former because he wrote too soon and too extravagantly, the latter because he also wrote too soon, retained a commitment to methodological objectivity of a sort, and turned his hand to practical human problems. And Rorty will almost certainly fail because of the scope of his historicism.

But Rorty is not writing too soon. If we look beyond professional philosophy, and even beyond other academic disciplines, the issue is less one of possible Rortyan influence, and more one of actual Rortyan summation of a view already current. The historicism of the social scientist or the literary critique has only a slight lead on that of the general "intellectual" population in North America and Europe. Nietzsche and Dewey offered metanarratives for which we were not ready. But Rorty is writing when all that is needed to understand him is in place, namely, the impatience with correspondism and foundationalism, which Bernstein tries to construe as the beginning of a wholesale revision of rationality, and which professional philosophers describe as facile or pernicious relativism. To many people—largely outside philosophy—Rorty's vision is neither disturbing nor problematic. It is simply overdue—and even lagging—recognition of our historicity. Nor is it surprising that philosophers should here appear to lag, since their primary arrogance has been to imagine that they had the edge on ultimate, and hence ahistorical, knowledge.

We seem to have, then, a contrast between a conservative professional group and the bulk of our society, a contrast which may limit the productiveness of Rorty's critique, since the conservative will not listen and the nonconservative thinks he has heard it all before. So we might be tempted to think, as several commentators do, that Rorty has only rejected traditional empiricist foundationalism and the professionalized school of philosophy it spawned through transformations into positivism and "analysis." This would be to take Rorty's notion of capital-P Philosophy as applying only to certain already discredited schools of thought. It is also to reconstrue the historicist mood outside philosophy as excessive because it is still in flux in reaction to the bad sort of foundationalism. Philosophers would then be in the enviable and usual position of being ahead of the pack in trying to assimilate the fallibilist/historicist insights available since Hegel into the sound mainstream philosophical tradition. The apparent gap between professional philosophers and everybody else would not result from philosophers lagging, but from their engagement in synthesizing the bulk of our intellectual tradition and what is important in historicist thinking. I do not think this is right. First, Rorty's critique has greater scope and power than the view in question allows. In that sense philosophical conservatism is evident in the attempt to narrow the scope of criticism to what has already been abandoned. Second, Rorty is surely correct that the professional philosopher has no exclusive ground on which to stand against the whole of culture and history. Nonetheless, the conservative philosophical view of Rorty is not *just* wrong or hopelessly reactionary. There is something to the claim that Rorty unfairly ignores a viable continuity and progress in both philosophy in particular and culture in general. To this extent he rejects what has already been abandoned, and to this extent the philosopher does seem to be in a special position with respect to assessing what has happened—if only because lack of particularized expertise forces on her a certain breadth of vision. Rorty seems wrong in not granting that culture and history may be becoming "singular" in the sense that Habermas and Nielsen want rationality to be singular. The very fact that our historicity is now seen so readily poses a problem for Rorty, as I want now to demonstrate. I shall begin by suggesting a sense in which philosophy is over.

HOW PHILOSOPHY IS OVER

We must be careful in our discussion of the end of traditional philosophy. Detail of presentation is less important than establishing the right perspective on what is a simple but still elusive point. We must show how Rorty's historicist critique of fundamental philosophical principles changes the nature of philosophy.

It could be argued that philosophy ended with Nietzsche, or with Dewey, but that argument would be difficult to sustain, given the subsequent rise of logical positivism, "ordinary language" philosophy, "conceptual analysis," and so on. However, the sense in which philosophy might have ended with Nietzsche or Dewey, and more likely has ended with Rorty, is quite compatible with people continuing to philosophize.

This paradoxical point is usually missed in Rorty's contentions. At least in my interpretation, his claim that the end of philosophy should be recognized is not the claim that philosophizing has stopped or will stop. It is a claim about the status of philosophizing.

In order to clarify how philosophy may be over, I want to use as a point of departure a notion suggested to me by Arthur Danto's claim that *art* is over.[9] As I understand it, Danto does not maintain that people no longer do art. Many mistakenly think that they refute Danto's claim by indicating the persistence of creative activity, and they resent what they also mistake as Danto's preclusion of new art. But Danto does not rule out new *works* of art. He does not argue, as some do, that there is nothing new and important to be done. The claim that art is over is not merely a conservative and sentimental rejection of contemporary efforts in favor of some period's masterpieces. Danto's claim has to do with the matter of the *nature* of art. And in the same way, the end of philosophy that Rorty preaches has to do not with philosophizing but with the nature of philosophizing.

Imagine a time when only works of painting and sculpture were considered art, even though other things might have been called works of art in an extended and commendatory way. That would mean that a painting or piece of sculpture, as the product of deliberate activity, would be a special sort of artifact. As that special sort of artifact, it would be either a good or a bad work of art—but it would not be *only* an artifact. Just as a paragraph or sentence is deemed to have meaning in an inherent way, and is not considered a paragraph or sentence at all if nonsensical, a painting or piece of sculpture would be deemed a work of art in an inherent way, irrespective of its aesthetic merit. If it lacked artistic value, it would be a bad painting or sculpture; if it had artistic worth, it would be a good painting or sculpture. The worst criticism would be to say that it was not art at all, just as a nonsensical sentence is not a sentence at all, but only gibberish. To say the thing in question was not art would be to reduce it to the status of an ordinary artifact, no matter how cunningly constructed.

If in a context like the one just sketched, someone claimed, after playing a few melodies, that music was an art form and the melodies works of art, there would be much debate about whether the category "art" included orchestrated sound. And the issue would be thought one of fact, the answer to which must be discerned, rather than decided. We saw a similar debate some decades ago with respect to whether photography was an art form. It is in this sense that art is over. There is no longer a category of special artifacts or activities. The question "Is this art?" cannot arise anymore, except as a question about an honorific use of the term "art." There has been something like a loss of innocence; it is now considered hopelessly naive to think there can be preexisting criteria—no matter how elusive—for what is art.

But it is not art as an activity that is over; it is art as a *kind*. It is no longer possible to affirm or deny the status of any product of human activity as a work of art, that is, to judge that it does or does not belong in the determinate category "art." The distinction has been eradicated between criteria for inclusion in a class and evaluatory criteria. The "end" of art has to do with the recognition that there simply is no meaningful way to define a category "art," for there are no means to exclude anything from it. Even products of nonhuman processes or chance events may be deemed works of art without serious conceptual penalties if attention is called to them in a special way and the artifact aspect is waived or suspended. For example, if someone successfully placed a red sphere in orbit beyond Pluto and then claimed the entire solar system as a piece of sculpture, we might debate whether or not the ploy succeeded, whether it was interesting or boring, whether or not we liked it. But it would be pointless—and primitive—to argue about whether it was art. That question was finished with Andy Warhol's soup can, or any of a hundred other cases in point.

Once the question of whether something is art can no longer be asked—because the sortal category has been replaced with an honorific one—the exciting time of putative *discovery* is ended, and we enter an equally exciting time of acknowledged *invention*. The artist is no longer conceived as identifying and wresting truth or value from some Platonic realm by producing works of an inherently special sort. Rather the artist is thought to be enhancing culture. Artistry then consists in contributing *well*, as opposed to instantiating something of a unique sort. One can, of course, choose to contribute within the limits of the sonnet or classical symphony. But one can also create freely, and perhaps invent new *genres*. The exercise of artistry becomes the exercise of specially refined skill and creativity. And the question asked of the products of artistry is not "Is this art?" but "Does this enrich us?"

Since Rorty has challenged philosophy's correspondist and foundationalist presuppositions, showed us that philosophy is not the culmination of a unique method of abstract thought gestating since Plato, and established that "analysis" is no more fundamental a methodology than phenomenology or taoism, we cannot ask of something "Is this philosophy?" That question does not make sense anymore, for we now understand how it can *always* be answered in the affirmative, by providing the appropriate historical context, and how it can *always* be answered in the negative, by assuming some methodology as fundamental and some judgments as apodictic.

As "art" ceased to be the name of an activity and its products, marked off from other activities and products by inherent value or unique properties, so "philosophy" ceased to be the name of an activity and its products, marked off from other activities and products by its more perfect embodiment of ahistorical rationality and discernment of the greatest truths. There is no more art in the sense of *just this* activity and *just these* products, and there is no more philosophy in the sense of *just this* sort of thought and *just these* conclusions. But creative, nonutilitarian enhancement of culture has not ceased, and thought about how things hang together has not ceased. The initiation of new *genres* in both art and philosophy also persists, for others can always closely emulate the novel efforts of a given artist or philosopher. All that has ended is the necessity to judge creative activity in art or philosophy as either conforming to, or falling short of, instantiated ideals. The fact that some people continue to do art or philosophy with the old assumptions, taking themselves to be engaged in unique activities and producing works with unique properties, changes nothing. The cardinal point is that their efforts can now be construed historically. There is no longer any compulsion—through lack of viable options—to grant the claimed special nature of art or the *a priori* nature of philosophy.

Art ended when works of art of varying kinds proliferated beyond any semblance of conformity to established categories. It became evident that a work of art was not something that satisfied certain preexisting criteria, but rather something we were willing to *count* as a work of art, to which we would grant special merit and status. Nietzsche and Dewey produced category-defying works that were still inescapably philosophical in their scope and implications while both failing to conform to, and criticizing, philosophical canons. However, the lesson was not learned, for reasons about which we can only speculate. Rorty has made the lesson inescapable not only by producing philosophy that is not capital-P Philosophy and articulating and explicitly challenging traditional philosophical assumptions and presuppositions, but also by keeping his critique free of vitiating positive theses such as Nietzsche's and lingering problematic commitments such as Dewey's.

But to acknowledge that philosophy is over—recognized as not being a natural kind, to put the point in Rorty's favorite way—in that it can no longer be considered a single discipline concerned with limning the rational universe, is not to acknowledge that thinking about how things hang together amounts to authoring metanarratives on a par with one another as well as with their object-narratives. As there is growth in scientific knowledge, our philosophical narratives and metanarratives may prove more and more durable and become less and less amenable to narrational restructuring, not because of "conceptual" necessity or a privileged methodology, but because they approach being empirically *right*—that is, not as narratives and metanarratives of a special "conceptual" sort, but as very high level scientific hypotheses in the broadest sense of "scientific."

Rorty rejects the category of "the conceptual" as picking out a special activity, but he also rejects that of "the scientific." He is willing to grant greater or lesser efficacy to narratives, discourses or metaphor-sets. I am trying to state here what I suggested earlier: Rorty cannot *preclude* their achieving a degree of efficacy that resists displacement by competitors because of its (contingent) correctness, and there is no *a priori* reason to exclude philosophical narratives from such achievement. It might be further noted that, given the creatures we are, there are limits to our narrational inventiveness; and that, given the world, there are limits to the variety of efficacious narratives or metaphor-sets. And if that is granted, it is granted that the world can be better or worse described, and that there can be growth in knowledge.

But if philosophy is over in the manner suggested—if it *never was* what it claimed to be—what of Davidson and Williams? What sort of enterprise are they engaged in, and what is it I am doing in this book? This is probably the toughest question raised by Rorty. We may appreciate his therapeutic influence and therefore overlook his extreme historicism, but if we grant that he is right about capital-P Philosophy, how are we to describe even his project and our evaluation of it?

We begin with the lack of set procedures or identifiable method. Aside from ultimately too vague proposals about careful analysis, dialectic, and so on, philosophy has seldom had—or had for long—established procedures that might serve to define a unique discipline. What comes to mind are such things as the infamous paradigm-case argument and the Positivists' Verification Principle, both of which led to more discussion in their rejection than to anything like positive results. "Analysis of meaning" was, for a time, the closest philosophers came to having a learnable, repeatable practice that could plausibly constitute the core of a unique discipline. And even then it was hard to see what could exclude perceptive and disciplined chemists or economists from the practice. Rorty is not personally responsible for making us see that there really is no such thing as capital-P Philosophy; he quite rightly gives the credit to others, mainly Quine and Sellars.

Davidson is certainly doing philosophy, and his disciplinary preparation was certainly specialized. But his philosophizing is not an instance of a natural kind any more than Victor Passmore's painting is. It is, in fact, very difficult to say just what it is that some philosophers consider special about what Davidson does; what they hold out for with respect to their discipline, beyond the real progress claimed against Rorty by any discipline. When this is realized, it emerges that the way philosophy was thought to be a natural kind had to do with *necessity*. The essential idea was that people were philosophizing when they were discerning the most fundamental truths. Davidson wants to be right, but he does not think he is right or is becoming right because he has somehow broken through to a level of actuality below the causal. An anonymous and well-known late medieval woodcut shows a man breaking through a dome containing the sun, stars, and the earth on which he is kneeling, and gazing at a realm of perfect spheres. That is the self-image of the philosopher. But it has never been very clear by what means the philosopher is supposed to achieve perception of ultimate reality. In effect, proper philosophy was just *whatever* led to the discernment of fundamental, necessary truths.

It was thought for a time that "conceptual analysis" was the quintessential philosophical technique, and that it could be done *independently* of anything else—such as historical or scientific accounts of how we came to have the concepts we have. Some concepts were thought basic to being rational. The idea was that elemental concepts, such as those of mind or voluntary action, were stable enough to admit of analysis and to support conclusions specially characterized by "conceptual necessity." *That* is what is over. Davidson, rather than doing that sort of philosophy, has as his basic project the demonstration that there is no *one* thing that is language, and therefore no material for such analysis or support for such certainty. Philosophy has to do with rigor, discipline, and, especially, abstractness. It concerns what Sellars describes as seeing, in the most general way, how things hang together, in the most general way. And philosophy must be capable of success and progress, as any sort of inquiry is, not because it adequately maps a conceptual reality; its success must result from better mapping *reality*, from saying how things *do* hang together.

METANARRATIVES

In the last chapter I spoke of the delineability of discourses as an obstacle to Rorty's contentions. An initial clarification is called for here. Whether discourses are seen as diverse, or as continuous, largely determines whether one construes historicity as in some sense total, as Rorty does, or as limited, in allowing a measure of retrospective objectivity, as I want to. The required clarification concerns just what we are calling "continuous" or "discontinuous."

Clearly there are what we might call *dialects* that are markedly distinct one from another. For instance, the working jargon of physicists will differ from that of retailers or graphic artists. Davidson's notion of a "passing theory," of a particular, developed linguistic practice, might be the most useful one for describing how participants in an enterprise develop dialects.[10] But these dialects, though they may incorporate distinctive metaphors, do not constitute different *discourses*. Any individual will use several dialects, and, unless we want to postulate conceptual schizophrenia, the kinds of differences among Rortyan discourses are not differences among dialects. Rorty has in mind discourses generated by what Stephen Pepper might have called root-metaphors: ways of speaking and thinking that shape and condition what we do and say, not just in specialized pursuits but in an overall way. For example, consider the differences between the thought and conversation of a sixteenth-century theistic serf and a twentieth-century atheistic technician. Those differences are not explicable in terms of varying dialects. The operant metaphor-sets are much more basic, and broader in scope, than those underlying dialects—though the latter may be cumulatively equivalent. Dialects are perhaps best described as specialized implementations of metaphor-sets.

Rorty's discourses, vocabularies, or metaphor-sets must differ in ways that allow new ones to create objectives and values that were impossible in the old discourses, vocabularies, or metaphor-sets. Novelty of purpose—setting out to deconstruct a tradition or to see if quarks exist—must be attributable to new possibilities opened up by new vocabularies or metaphors. It cannot be a product of incremental progress, for if it were that progress would leave no room for the kind of "poetic" creativity and novelty Rorty emphasizes in his characterization of edifying thought. If Bloom's strong poet is the Rortyan hero, that poet provides us with something truly new; she initiates a new conversation, or creates new metaphors, that enables us to do things we did not dream of before. In Rorty's view, a Newton or an Einstein is a strong poet in this sense, for each supposedly initiated a new Rortyan conversation and thereby enabled us to construe the world and our practices in such a manner that "momentum" became an explanatory notion and a general field theory became an objective. Unlike Kuhn's paradigm shifts, which occur at least in part because theories collapse under the weight of qualifications, new conversations are *invented*. As for contemporaneous diversity, an Azande shaman and a nuclear physicist differ in that each employs a different vocabulary and participates in a different conversation; each copes with the world in terms of different elements and configurations of elements, and each uses and tolerates different principles governing those configurations. Against this, Williams would see Einstein's "conversation" as an evolution of Newton's, and as having to incorporate much that was efficacious in Newton's. As for the shaman's way of coping, Williams would consider it inherently less reliable and efficacious than ours.

What saves the Rortyan picture from being conceptual-scheme pluralism, aside from Rorty's avowed rejection of the scheme/content distinction, is that the metaphor-sets or vocabularies are not relative *to* anything, namely, to different underlying ostensions or differently arranged ostensions. Rorty does not want to relate vocabularies to the world as true descriptions, and he must guard against relating them to anything "internal," such as different phenomenal givens. The efficacy or productivity of discourses or metaphor-sets must be "absolute" in the sense mentioned earlier: they work as they do because they work as they do, not because they more or less approximate true description or because they are generated by particularly useful ostensions.

Put in terms of Rortyan conversations, the putative end of philosophy— or of what Rorty designates capital-P Philosophy—is, roughly, the end of the Plato-Descartes-Dummett conversation, because that conversation is deemed less interesting and productive now than its competitors. The way to philosophize now is to take part in the Hegel-Dewey-Rorty conversation. The difference here is allegedly between being thought, and not being thought, to escape time and history. However, that is a very sharp distinction. And it makes us wonder about the perspicacity we have achieved just by being able to characterize the options in question. Rorty undoubtedly sees that perspicacity as a central support of his view, but it actually poses a problem for him. Nielsen, in discussing the possible progress of philosophy, sums up the point as follows:

> [N]o matter how much we may be attracted to [Rortyan] end-of-philosophy theses, Habermas is surely right in stressing with Hegel that our historical experience is such that we can no longer accept a

naive consensus. We . . . are aware of too many different ways of life,
points of view, universes of discourse, conflicting ideologies, to possibly just naively accept the doing of the things done in our society.
    This 'experience of reflection', as Hegel calls it, quite naturally
inclines us to what Lyotard calls metanarratives.[11]

The "metanarratives" explain why and how we relate our beliefs and
practices within societal, cultural, or epochal contexts to beliefs and
practices outside those contexts. There are philosophers who want some of
those external beliefs and practices to be transcendent, to constitute
rational matrices, but they need not; they may constitute only what I
described as retrospectively objective standards. But the point I want to
make here is that once we have metanarratives, once we encompass
belief-networks and practices in larger ones having some explanatory
power, we seem to have bases for reflection very different from Rorty's
individual vocabularies or metaphor-sets. What we have, in effect, is the
wherewithal to form relative judgments *about* metaphor-sets or
vocabularies—always assuming these can in fact be sufficiently differentiated. In this way, our very awareness and acceptance of our historicity
elevate historical reflection in a significant, though admittedly not very
clear, manner. We seem, then, not so much to escape time or history but
to come to an understanding of history that is too large to be just another
story—unless we tolerate the idea of open-ended extendability with
respect to our metanarratives.
    Rorty would respond that there is simply no accessible difference, no
way of telling whether a metanarrative achieves the sort of retrospective
objectivity I am arguing for, or whether it is just broader than the last and
less inclusive than the next. But I do not consider the matter quite so hopeless. Historical perspicacity poses for Rorty the problem of how to explain
consistent productivity and explanatory coincidence at the metanarrative
level. If we are now too sophisticated to accept "local" narratives and
practices as "in order"—the way Wittgensteinian language games are "in
order" just in being played—if we have learned from Marx and Freud,
and if we are now actively concerned with seeing how "local" narratives
and practices hang together with other current and earlier ones, can we
simply be constructing new and ever more encompassing metanarratives
that differ from others only in scope of inclusion? I think the central issue
here is one of credibility: How far can we go before we must admit the
applicability of the idea of *correctness* to our stories? Rorty answers: As far
as human history may take us.
    Rorty views metanarratives as basically justificatory; they are stories we

tell about discourses in order to defend or change those discourses (see note 11). Metanarratives, then, will be more or less novel, more or less productive, but they will not differ in kind from the object-narratives they deal with. They will not be more accurately descriptive or well-grounded than the object-narratives. Our sophistication, then, is just more of the same. At most it will be more perspicacious storytelling, storytelling that encompasses more of what we do and have done, and that does so more self-consciously. In this way, the history of science and much of the philosophy of science are a complex story about Aristotle, Galileo, Newton, and Einstein, designed to make Einstein look especially good.

For Rorty metanarratives do not and cannot constitute or exhibit growth in knowledge. If they impress us with their breadth, complexity, and sophistication, if they seem to make "objective" sense of large chunks of human activity, it is only because we put into them what we then deem to be discernment of the "actuality" of trains of events. Any given metanarrative may be displaced at any time by a new metanarrative that will claim greater perspicacity and accuracy. Of course, this point is made at a very high and abstract level, which has nothing to do with ongoing practices and mundane talk. The ordinary operant beliefs in truth and objectivity are not disturbed; life goes on. In fact, few can be expected to understand or fully appreciate the alleged totality of our historicity. After all, Jean-Paul Sartre's vision of how we are morally on our own was not universally accepted and stopped few people from relying on their ethical institutions. But philosophers must get the message.

The end of philosophy has to do with metanarratives because philosophers are notoriously the most ambitious metanarrativists. And they claim either apodictic truth or "conceptual" truth for their narratives. While those metanarratives are no longer advanced as instances of the near-completion of knowledge, as were Plato's and Leibniz's, they are still proffered as having achieved an imposing measure of clarity, as in the case of Ryle and Dummett. Moreover, these metanarratives have achieved such clarity because they are products of a *special* activity: Philosophy. However, even if we side with Williams and Nielsen in our belief that Rorty is wrong about the growth of knowledge and that some metanarratives assume proportions too outsized for them to be *just* stories—though we are not quite sure how—we need not endorse the idea that philosophy is a special discipline that belongs on the "real growth" side of the ledger. Put differently, we do not understand how some narratives or metanarratives can be only stories, but just because we are academic philosophers, we need not automatically count philosophical narratives and metanarratives among those manifesting progress. We may want to construe philosophy as Rorty and Sellars do, as the most abstract and general sort of rigorous inquiry into how things hang together in the broadest sense.

Rorty does not want to tolerate the idea of possible variance between efficaciousness and truth. He thinks that, aside from mundane uses, "true" becomes an otiose notion once we can describe our discourses or parts of our discourses as, say, "warranted assertible." But what *makes* something a "warranted assertible" proposition, instead of a true one, is internal to a discourse. No metaphor-set, discourse, or conversation can be inherently better than another. Yet Rorty does not want to deny differences in productivity or efficacy, so he attributes these to discourses or metaphor-sets in some complete way, and in effect translates greater efficacy or productivity into a novelty allowing of new purposes and new means to attain those purposes. We, his critics, maintain that, beyond a certain point, efficaciousness and truth cannot vary, not because they are identical but because the former establishes the latter, and the differences in productivity among discourses are due to degree of correctness. We are obviously drawing a different "moral," for there is no question of establishing that we are right. Our strongest point seems to be the question, How can we accept overwhelming consistency and productivity as an "accidental" consequence of a given metaphor-set or discourse? Rorty, in answering, must be careful not to overemphasize the idea that a discourse or metaphor-set in large part determines its own goals and standards for productivity. This is an implicit Rortyan contention, but it is an extremely dangerous one, for it supports the charge that Rortyan pragmatism is idealist in nature.

What we have, then, is our unwillingness to deny or ignore growth in knowledge, against Rorty's overly democratic view of the status and interrelatedness of our discourses or enterprises. But it is not at all clear that in defending the growth of knowledge we must also defend philosophy as a unique discipline.

CONCLUSION

Rorty has consolidated and refined a pragmatic critique of traditional philosophy that began with Nietzsche and continued, in varying degrees, with James, Dewey, Quine, and others. By focusing on analytic philosophy and writing in the present time, Rorty engages the strongest and most refined expression of philosophical thought and methodology. Rorty's previous mastery of analytic philosophy strengthens his critique. But his influence and success will be determined by whether Rorty's views are adequately recognized and adopted. We may agree that current interest in his work reflects a commitment to an historicist alternative to the traditional conception of philosophy as universal and ahistorical, but the question is whether Rorty will be "taken up," whether *his* alternative will be adopted, or whether it will ultimately be counted among philosophical peculiarities, such as occasionalism. Rorty can fail if his vision becomes a *topic* of esoteric conversation, rather than a *shaper* of conversation. Even rejection of his extreme historicism with respect to progress in inquiry need not preclude his influence. But if his construal of philosophy as only very abstract inquiry (and not special discipline with a special methodology) is rejected, his influence is nullified.

The many articles on Rorty and reviews of his work indicate that he is presently the subject of much discussion.[12] But the crucial question is *how* he is discussed. Even if we are likely to decide that, given fallibilism and historicism, we will defend a view of rationality that incorporates a minimum of objectivity—the sort of retrospective objectivity I think now evident in our very historicity—discussion of Rorty can be productive. I want to close this chapter by considering how Rorty may best influence philosophers, and by offering a final articulation of how retrospective objectivity limits pragmatism.

In her "An Historicist View of Teaching Philosophy," Lisa Portmess illustrates the best sort of Rortyan influence. She takes Rorty as her point of departure in considering the divergence between teaching philosophy as comprising universal problems, and teaching it as comprising historically and culturally rooted problems.[13] Portmess describes the main consequences of the two approaches: the former "encourages the student to view philosophies of other cultures and eras through his or her own tradition," while the latter "stresses the changing cultural and historical character of philosophical problems and . . . asks the student to go outside his or her tradition."[14] Portmess adds that

> The first view, that philosophical problems are universal and time-less, is pervasive in our culture. This view is reflected in the mode of teaching of most professors of philosophy and in nearly every anthology . . . which groups its readings from different eras and cultures around general philosophical topics such as the foundations

of knowledge. . . . This is a view which . . . recognizes a diversity of answers but a common core of questions, and a common program for . . . inquiry.[15]

Rorty's work afforded Portmess the intellectual provocation to see that how she was taught philosophy, and how she had been teaching philosophy, was only one way of doing so. Rorty's work enabled her to realize that if the answers to philosophical problems vary among cultures and historical periods, perhaps the problems differ; perhaps "philosophical problems appear, disappear, change shape, according to new assumptions and new vocabularies."[16]

Rorty's critique of traditional philosophy legitimized Portmess's own reservations arising from her experience studying at Duke University in North Carolina and Queen's University in Canada, and teaching at the American University of Beirut and Gettysburg College in Pennsylvania. She was struck by the distortions resulting from the assumption that philosophical problems are ahistorical and acultural. When philosophy is so taught, students invariably find it remote from their lives and interests and approach it as something of an oddity, as the sort of intellectual subject that demands a nodding acquaintance but will never be of use or real concern. This latter point illustrates how philosophizing becomes enshrined as capital-P Philosophy, for if one is introduced to very abstract rigorous inquiry as concern with an ahistorical set of problems and an equally ahistorical methodology grounded in necessary truth, failure to understand philosophical problems so construed, or to appreciate their supposed import, will be attributed to one's own shortcomings, not to large-scale misconception of the enterprise. The result is a sacrosanct "discipline" that is vaguely revered but practically ignored and left to its own priesthood.

In my view, the important realization forced by Rorty's work is that the ahistoricist position is impossible. That is, it becomes clear on reflection that philosophizing *cannot* be free of time and history; the articulation of, and responses to, philosophical problems are embedded in history. We simply cannot achieve the necessary neutrality. For one thing, historicist construals of philosophical issues will always be available; the only way such construals could be systematically discounted would be to beg the question against them by arguing that they are *mis*construals of ahistorical issues. Proving that philosophy is ahistorical is a matter of proving a negative: that problems and proposed answers are *not* products of "local" cultural and historical conditions and the effects of those conditions on philosophers. But all of this is true of *doing* philosophy, of the *production* of philosophy, where philosophizing is inquiry at the most general level but may be misconceived as apodictic reasoning or a limning of the world of Forms. The same things need not be true of the historical consideration of philosophy—or of science or literature—from a sufficiently abstract perspective. Rorty's success in calling attention to the historicist nature of philosophy is not necessarily success in showing the total historicity of all surveys of human knowledge and enterprise, regardless of their time and the attendant scope of their purview.

Portmess may be authoring a metanarrative, but it is one that, in trying to give full weight to history and culture, differs in an important way from "first order" involvement with issues. That difference may not itself amount to objectivity, retrospective or any other sort, but it is a difference that demands understanding in terms other than either "first order" or "second order" authoring, where the latter differs only in that its objects of discourse are instances of the former. Portmess is not just philosophizing about philosophizing, as philosophizing may be epochal thought about justice or immortality. Portmess makes certain judgments, for instance, that have a peculiarly special character. She reminds us that "It may indeed be that common themes and universal concerns are to be found in the philosophical writings of different peoples—themes of justice, or immortality, or skepticism about knowledge." But she cautions that

> the formulation of what is . . . problematic about a given theme may be only superficially the same across centuries and cultures . . . . What is gained . . . by a universalistic perspective . . . is a feeling of confidence in approaching that which would otherwise be strange and formidable. What is lost . . . is the vital connection of philosophy to culture and history.[17]

It is the awareness and articulation of options that impresses us here and amounts to a special perspicacity. A review of philosophy in diverse cultures and times, such as Portmess undertakes, indicates that philosophers have never succeeded individually in escaping their historical and cultural contexts. If anything, it appears that the more adamantly philosophers have insisted that they did so—the more they have argued that their thought captured timeless and apodictic truth, structure, or method—the more obvious it has been to later scholars that they failed in that respect. But it is precisely in realizing that point that we should realize how far we have come in understanding the way time and history shape our thought. Consider another passage from Portmess's article:

> The conception of "will" or the idea of the individual for a Chinese Confucianist, a European medievalist or a Muslim mystic are not fully comprehensible apart from the context from which they derive. Fertile river plain, mercantile city, desert expanse—each context leaves its stamp upon the philosophical ideas which emerge from it . . . . the historicist view helps to make comprehensible *why* Confucius was concerned with the relation of individuals to the state, or *why* Ibn Rushd was so concerned to defend the prerogatives of the philosopher against those who wished to subordinate philosophy to scripture.[18]

Admittedly, the recognition of the influence of history and culture on philosophizing is *itself* a product of history and culture. It is almost certain that Rorty would not have written as he has, or achieved the attention he has, if he had written in the 1890s instead of the 1980s, or in present-day Iran instead of North America, or perhaps as a latter-day Eric Hoffer instead of as a Princeton philosopher. But this point cuts both ways. It suggests that even retrospective metanarratives are the products of their time, but more importantly it suggests that their scope is contingent on their history. Nor is the latter the empty notion that the more history to survey, the greater the scope of a metanarrative. Rather, the implication is that the amount of history, and especially the amount of historical diversity, to be surveyed determines the nature of retrospective metanarratives. Rorty would have us believe that we will never achieve a position from which we can observe our history and be sure that no new construal will change our view of that history. But I do not think we are that clever or that creative, or that history—and especially the world—tolerates such a variety of construal. At least we must acknowledge the importance of the *kind* of history being surveyed. If, as in the case of science, there is a special and theoretically complex integration of the various stages surveyed, it may be superficial to conclude that each successive stage is a *new* stage, and essentially discontinuous with its predecessors.

The passages I have selected from Portmess illustrate more than

Rortyan influence. They also show that it is very difficult to imagine how change might continue indefinitely *in kind*—not in detail—with respect to the sort of thing Portmess is up to. As we progress, our range of diversity of historical construal narrows, so that changes become changes of narrower and narrower focus. Rorty is even willing to allow that capital-P Philosophy could be refurbished, that it might change back to what we had before—albeit with some enhancement.[19] He thinks such refurbishment would be only *another* epoch from the pragmatic point of view. I believe that such refurbishment would be a mistake, a "failure of nerve" in Gilbert Murray's sense.[20] It would ignore hard lessons learned. It would be *wrong* to reembrace ahistoricism.

Portmess provides an example of someone who has been liberated by Rorty's critique. By gaining enough distance and tolerance to understand the limitations of her methodology and that viable alternatives exist, she has been enriched in a manner Rorty values. She has become a full participant in a new conversation, one that gives real voices to what were at best only objects of discourse. But surely that sort of enrichment, that broadening, cannot continue indefinitely. Portmess must be able to say: I am wiser now; my understanding of philosophical problems is better. But she must lose some of what she has gained if she adds: Of course, I may change again. The trouble is the change must be a change for the *better*. If it is just a change, and if it is always a prelude to further change of the same order, "for the better" loses its significance. To put things differently, and in the way Williams and so many others have done, what can "for the better" mean if change is *always* possible, and if the change is from one to another discourse of equal value or efficacy?

Rorty has a tight circle going, and here I can offer no handy quotation other than one I recall from conversation. When asked what "productive" meant with respect to a discourse or vocabulary, he answered "It gets us what we want." But *what we want* is a function of our discourse or vocabulary. For example, scientists came to want a general field theory when they learned the discourse of particle physics. A general field theory could not be wanted in Newtonian science. So the Einsteinian conversation is more productive. How? It creates, and goes some way toward satisfying, new wants. We want, and can get, *more* than in Newton's discourse. Is the Einsteinian discourse *better* than the Newtonian? No—it is only richer in a way that has made us downgrade the other. This is just not enough—not because it can be shown to fall short of some standard, but because the notion of rationality and progress it offers is not very attractive. At the very least we feel there are discourses and discourses.

We may be prepared to allow great latitude with respect to literature and philosophy when it comes to ongoing reconstrual; we may not be prepared to allow as much in the case of history and science. The latter two enterprises—and especially science—now have contents too integrated and substantial to allow attribution of their present productivity and explanatory power to anything less than some minimal measure of correctness. In denying this minimal correctness, the *Rortyan* conversation looks less than productive—at least less so than an historicist one that allows some room for real progress, however that is to be understood. Rorty's conversation, which promises discursive civility and all the other Socratic virtues, fails miserably if, in a real sense, we have nothing to talk *about*. And that happens if the Rortyan perspective makes all subjects of discourse less than serious because they are always recognized as only products of a discourse, and therefore explorable only within the confines of their discourse. This is what Caputo meant by saying that Rorty reduces conversation to "just talk." We might as well just sit back and wait for the next strong poet.

It is a real question whether we *can* be Rortyan pragmatists, whether we can breathe the rarefied air of total historicity. Rorty himself notes that the deep objection to pragmatism is "the criticism that the Socratic virtues cannot, as a practical matter, be defended save by Platonic means," that we are unable to proceed without arguing for truth and objectivity.[21] Speaking of James's remark that life *feels* like a fight for real success and progress, for growth in knowledge and some measure of permanent achievement, Rorty says:

> For us, footnotes to Plato that we are, it *does* feel that way. But if James's own pragmatism were taken seriously, if pragmatism became central to our culture and our self-image, then it would no longer feel that way. We do not know how it *would* feel. We do not even know whether . . . the conversation . . . might not falter and die away. We just do not know. James and Dewey offered us no guarantees. They simply pointed to the situation we stand in, now that both the Age of Faith and the Enlightenment seem beyond recovery.[22]

Rorty of course hopes—and must believe—that the conversation will not falter, but he adds that "We did not change the course of conversation in the way [James and Dewey] suggested . . . . Perhaps we are still unable to . . . perhaps we never shall be able to."[23]

Perhaps we can understand the possibilities Nietzsche and Dewey offered only when we are defeated in the grand ahistoricist enterprise. As Portmess observes, the universalistic and ahistoricist conception of philosophy makes "the strange and formidable" seem manageable. In this way, correspondism and foundationalism are ironically and paradoxically pragmatic ways of coping. They enable us to deal with what would otherwise overwhelm us, or at least rob us of any impetus to do much more than survive. Without them most of us might indeed not be able to do more than wait for the next strong poet, and only a few among us who have really learned the lessons of history—Nietzsche, Dewey, Rorty— would be able to leave the Cave and look full on the Sun. Rorty speaks of honoring James and Dewey for offering us glimpses of how our lives might change, but even those glimpses may be available to too few.[24] It seems a paradigmatically pragmatic question to ask if so exclusive a perspective is productive. Pragmatism must remain a bleak and fruitless vision if its adoption requires heroism beyond the abilities of most of us, and its maintenance an almost religious purity and fervor.

The last point brings us to our conclusion: how pragmatism is, and must be, restricted. Rorty's therapeutic influence is unquestionable, and only a deep intellectual arrogance—or vanity—can support the conception of philosophy as a unique methodology available only to those with a talent and penchant for the apodictic and "conceptual." Even without Rorty's argument, professional philosophy has been ignored for decades by the rest of the intellectual community and has seen more and more of its practitioners defecting to "applied" ethics, socio-political metatheory, and so on. The few metaphysicians and epistemologists who persist are participants in a paradigmatic Rortyan conversation—one few others wish to join. But to conclude, how might we best articulate the sort of retrospective objectivity that I have been suggesting limits pragmatism and should limit Rorty's pragmatism?

We might begin by saying that Dewey's commitment to progress in inquiry was not at odds with his pragmatism; he understood the limits of the philosophical stance he championed, and which Rorty himself thinks Dewey stated so well. Dewey is right to agree with Peirce in *Logic* that the best use of intelligence leads to consensus, and that truth is just the consensus we reach when we get things right. Rorty will not accept that the nature of inquiry can ever achieve *correctness* about the world as its subject matter, so that for him consensus is never more than agreement on a current story. Rorty does not want our beliefs made true by anything; he just wants them to be useful. However we might wonder about the ultimate intelligibility of this distinction, we do want to be historicists and fallibilists, but we also want to insist that the efficacy of a discourse has to do with correctness. Still, we do not want to argue for Cartesian certainty. The question is how to phrase the conviction that when we engage in enough inquiry and achieve enough success, we must judge ourselves right, rather than lucky.

What I have been calling retrospective objectivity is not something *discerned*. It is a judgment—the judgment that after enough success and consistency in practice and prediction, a theoretical application works as it does because it *gets things right*. It will be obvious from what I have said that it must remain an open question whether what we lump together as the social sciences—and philosophical inquiry, however characterized— achieves the requisite degrees of success and consistency in practice and prediction. I am accepting that there is a basic difference, at least one not yet undermined, between the "hard" sciences—and now possibly history—and other forms of inquiry. I think, therefore, that Rorty's most serious error is to try to reduce science to just another discourse, to subsume it under the literary by making it another story.

Like Rorty, I have no demonstrative argument to offer here. I can only call attention to the crucial point that the only conception of an historicist rationality worth having or defending is one that differentiates among our enterprises and admits that some *are* descriptively successful, otherwise they could not work as they do.

The likeliest rebuttal is that my proposal is, after all, another story, another construal; it is essentially a way of looking at science, more decision than discernment. But that response is not likely to come from scientists. The trouble is that too many humanists have too vague an idea of geology or chemistry, let alone physics, to fully appreciate the extent of real knowledge presupposed by the control we now exercise. To think that the physical sciences constitute so many "stories" that might change radically with the introduction of a new metaphor is just naive. First, science, as a practice, is a myriad of tiny, focused projects. There is a science "story" only in the popularizer's Sunday Supplement articles or at a very high level where a small number of theorists manage to individually grasp most of the essentials of an area of scientific activity. For the science "story" or discourse to change as Rorty envisions—as the result of a new metaphor—we would need a revolution that is simply beyond comprehension. But it is not beyond comprehension because we have not *had* it; it is beyond comprehension because we do not know how to construe science as sufficiently unified to *be* a single story or discourse capable of holistic change. Second, Rorty seems largely indifferent to the fact that a great deal of physical science is couched in mathematics. Even if we allowed that the *interpretation* of the mathematical expressions of theories could change in light of a new metaphor, it is unclear how the mathematics could change. It is, after all, mathematics that enables the particle physicist to incorporate Newtonian mechanics, not the heuristic interpretation on either side of the equation.

As in earlier chapters we come to a modest conclusion—perhaps the best sort if we are trying to counter Rorty's contentions, which are anything but modest. We feel no compulsion to deny that some of the differences among our projects and enterprises have to do with the degree of correctness about the world that we sometimes achieve. We agree with Dewey that the best use of intelligence—disciplined and cooperative inquiry—must eventually achieve truth, in the sense that inquiry will result in practices of such efficacy and stability that we can only judge them so because of correctness. Inquiry may not achieve Cartesian certainty, but, always allowing that we might be wrong, it will achieve success explicable only in terms of descriptive correctness. And if we decide we are wrong at any point, it will be that we are *wrong*, not that we have abandoned one story for one we like better. Rorty's historicism, then, is too complete—unwarrantedly so, and unproductive.

As for philosophy, I think Rorty is right, but not surprisingly. The idea that philosophy survives as a special discipline after producing most of the other academic disciplines is unworkable. Once hardcore metaphysics and epistemology were precluded by everything from Positivism to poaching by cosmologists and psychologists, the "super science" view of philosophy began to look decidedly unconvincing. As for the idea that philosophy might continue as a sort of conceptual cartography, tracing the outlines of necessary boundries and relations among "meanings," if Quine, Sellars, Rorty, and others succeed at all, they succeed in exploding that myth. Mario Bunge might still attempt to produce "exact" philosophy by elaborating definitional matrices, but the professionalism of the 1960s—and all its assumptions—is over. Philosophers, aside from being what they are because of university administrative divisions, are only disciplined thinkers with a tradition of highly abstract inquiry and speculation, and with enough distance—and leisure—to look hard at the presuppositions of the sciences and near-sciences. If they teach anything unique, it is a restricted intellectual history. In any case, they do what they do not because it is a *special* activity but because they are willing, in the best Socratic tradition, to ask tough questions and are—a *little* like

judges—sufficiently removed from their object-disciplines to be reason-
ably detached from them. Philosophers are not the sons and daughters of
Plato, practitioners of an arcane science. Philosophers are, sometimes in
spite of themselves, the sons and daughters of Socrates. They are ques-
tioners.

Notes

1. John Locke, *An Essay Concerning Human Understanding*, in *Locke's Human Understanding*, A. S. Pringle-Pattison, ed. (London: Oxford, 1924; repr. 1964) 10.
2. See an interesting recent piece, Richard Rorty, "A Reply To Six Critics,"
which bears out my point about Rorty's modesty with respect to his own
contribution and clarifies his sense of "edifying philosophy," in *Analyse &
Kritik* 6 (1984): 78–98, especially 84–85.
3. Kai Nielsen, "Can There Be Progress in Philosophy?", forthcoming.
4. See Rorty, *Consequences*.
5. See, e.g., Taylor, "Minerva"; Levi, "Escape From Boredom"; Murphy,
Critical Notice of *Mirror*, Skinner, "The End of Philosophy?"; Schwartz,
Review of *Mirror*, Mannison, Review of *Consequences*.
6. What I have in mind here is exemplified by the response of a colleague,
Alistair MacLeod, to a paper I read on Rorty. MacLeod pressed the charges
of relativism and dubious use of language against Rorty by demanding of me
whether there was anything problematic about saying there were doughnuts
before us as we sat around a table drinking coffee and eating doughnuts. He
also linked to this "unproblematic" assertion the assertion that torture is bad.
I answered that there was nothing problematic about the first assertion, *except*
that its context made it necessary to hear a little more before saying so.
MacLeod would have none of that, claiming that discussion of anything
problematic, say of an epistemological sort, must come *after* the admission
that we could agree without reservations that there were indeed doughnuts on
the table. I do not think MacLeod, or others of like mind, take themselves to
be defending foundationalism. But the trouble is that they insist on the
existence of a level of discourse at which it makes no sense to have reservations
about the truth of what is said and at which interpretation is not operant.
Peter Hacker concurs in this "analytic" view by arguing that there are some
uses of language, like "Pass the salt," where there is no interpretation in the
sense that there is no Davidsonian "passing theory"—or any sort of theory—
operant. (See, for instance, his forthcoming "Rules and Pseudo-rules.") I
think these views are harmless if their point is that there are cases where
disputes simply do not arise in practice, and that we ought to reserve talk of
theories for more elaborate activities. But these views are not harmless if their
point is that perception and language are anchored in cases somehow elemental and "direct."
7. Rorty, *Consequences*, 173–74, 93–95.
8. Rorty, *Consequences*, xlii.

9. Arthur Danto, "Philosophy and the Disenfranchisement of Art," a lecture given on his visit to Queen's University, Kingston, Ontario, as a John Milton Scott Visitor, 3–5 October 1984. See also Danto's "The End of Art," in Berel Lang, *The Death of Art* (New York: Haven, 1984), 5–35, and Arthur Danto, *The Transfiguration of the Commonplace* (Cambridge: Harvard University Press, 1981).

10. See Davidson, "A Nice Derangement."

11. Nielsen, "Can There Be Progress," 16; see also Jurgen Habermas, "Questions and Counterquestions," in *Habermas and Modernity* (Cambridge: Cambridge University Press, 1985) 169–71, and Rorty's own characterization of meta-narratives in Richard Rorty, "Postmodernist Bourgeois Liberalism," *The Journal of Philosophy* 80 (1985): 585:

> [Metanrarratives are] narratives which describe . . . the activities of such entities as the noumenal self or the Absolute Spirit or the Proletariat. These . . . are stories which purport to justify loyalty to, or breaks with, certain contemporary communities.

12. See bibliography.

13. Lisa Portmess, "An Historicist View of Teaching Philosophy," *Teaching Philosophy* 7 (1984): 313–23. I chose this piece over a number of others partly because of a personal interest in Portmess's work. She was one of my most promising Ph.D. students, and while in Princeton I introduced her to Rorty and his work.

14. Ibid., 313.

15. Ibid.

16. Ibid., 313–14.

17. Ibid., 315.

18. Ibid.

19. Rorty, *Mirror*, 394.

20. Gilbert Murray, "The Failure of Nerve," in *Five Stages of Greek Religion*, 3d ed. (Garden City, N.Y.: Doubleday/Anchor, 1951), 119–65; see also Gilbert Murray, "Pagan Religion and Philosophy at the Time of Christ," in *Humanist Essays* (London: Allen and Unwin, 1964), 107–38.

21. Rorty, *Consequences*, 174.

22. Ibid., 174–75.

23. Ibid., 175.

24. Ibid.

Bibliography

Works referred or alluded to in text are marked with an asterisk.

*Armstrong, D. M. *A Materialist Theory of the Mind*. Routledge, Kegan Paul, 1968.

*Bernstein, Richard. "Philosophy in the Conversation of Mankind." *The Review of Metaphysics* 33 (1980): 745–76. (Review of *Mirror*)

*———. *Beyond Objectivism and Relativism: Science, Hermeneutics and Praxis*. University of Pennsylvania Press, 1983.

———. ed. *Habermas and Modernity*. Cambridge University Press, 1985.

*Bleicher, Josef. *Contemporary Hermeneutics: Hermeneutics as Method, Philosophy and Critique*. Routledge and Kegan Paul, 1980.

*Caputo, John, "The Thought of Being and the Conversation of Mankind: the Case of Heidegger and Rorty." *The Review of Metaphysics* 36 (1983): 661–85.

*Cavell, Stanley. *Must We Mean What We Say?* Scribner's, 1969.

*———. *The Claim of Reason: Wittgenstein, Skepticism, Morality and Tragedy*. Clarendon Press, 1979.

*Danto, Arthur. *The Transfiguration of the Commonplace*. Harvard, 1981.

*———. "The End of Art." In *The Death of Art*, edited by Berel Lang, 5–35, Haven, 1984.

*———. "Philosophy and the Disenfranchisement of Art." Lecture given at Queen's University, Kingston, Ontario, as a John Milton Scott Visitor, 3–5 October 1984.

*Davidson, Donald. "Truth and Meaning." *Synthese* 17 (1967): 304–23.

*———. "On the Very Idea of a Conceptual Scheme." *Proceedings of the American Philosophical Association* 17 (1973–74): 5–20.

*———. "A Coherence Theory of Truth and Knowledge." In *Kant oder Hegel?*, edited by Dieter Henrich, Klett-Cotta, 1983.

*———. *Inquiries into Truth and Interpretation*. Oxford University Press, 1984.

*_____. "A Nice Derangement of Epitaphs." Paper read at Queen's University, Kingston, Ontario, 27 September 1984. Forthcoming in Grandy, R., and R. Warner, eds. *Philosophical Grounds of Rationality: Intentions, Categories and Ends.* Oxford University Press.

*Dewey, John. *Essays in Experimental Logic.* University of Chicago, 1916. Reprint. Dover, 1966.

*_____. *Experience and Nature.* Open Court, 1929.

*_____. *Logic: The Theory of Inquiry.* Henry Holt, 1938.

*_____. *Experience and Nature.* 2d ed. Republication. Dover, 1958.

Dreyfus, Hubert. "Holism and Hermeneutics." *Review of Metaphysics* 34 (1980): 3–23.

Eldridge, Richard. "Philosophy and the Achievement of Community: Rorty, Cavell and Criticism." *Metaphilosophy* 14: 107–25.

*Feigl, Herbert, and Wilfrid Sellars, eds. *Readings in Philosophical Analysis.* Appleton-Century-Crofts, 1949.

*Gadamer, Hans-Georg. *Truth and Method.* Edited and translated by G. Barden and J. Cumming. Seabury Press, 1975.

*_____. *Philosophical Hermeneutics.* Edited and translated by David Linge. University of California Press, 1976.

*Habermas, Jurgen. "Questions and Counterquestions." In *Habermas and Modernity,* edited by Richard Bernstein. Cambridge University Press, 1985.

*Hacking, Ian. "On the Frontier." *The New York Review,* 20 December 1984.

*Jones, Peter. *Philosophy and the Novel.* Oxford University Press, 1975.

Langham, Paul. Review of *Philosophy in History. Canadian Philosophical Reviews* 5 (1985): 386–88.

Langiulli, Nino. Review of "Philosophy and the Mirror of Nature." *Interpretation* 13 (1985): 119–41.

*Levi, Isaac. "Escape from Boredom: Edification According to Rorty." *Canadian Journal of Philosophy* 11 (1981): 589–601.

*Locke, John. *An Essay Concerning Human Understanding.* In *Locke's Human Understanding,* edited by A. S. Pringle-Pattison. Oxford, 1924. Reprinted 1964.

*MacIntyre, Alisdair. "Philosophy, the 'Other' Disciplines, and Their Histories: A Rejoinder to Richard Rorty." *Soundings* 65: 127–145.

_____. "Epistemological Crises, Dramatic Narrative and the Philosophy of Science." *The Monist* 60 (1977): 453–72.

*McDermott, John J., R. W. Sleeper, and Abraham Edel. "Symposium on Rorty's

Consequences of Pragmatism." *Transactions of the Charles S. Peirce Society* 21 (1985): 1–39.

*Mannison, Donald. Review of *Consequences*. *Australasian Journal of Philosophy* 63 (1983): 96–8.

Margolis, Joseph. "Pragmatism Without Foundations." *American Philosophical Quarterly* 21 (1984): 69–80.

*Meynell, Hugo. "Reversing Rorty." Paper read at Queen's University, Kingston, Ontario, 6 December 1984. Forthcoming in *Method*.

*_____. "Scepticism Reconsidered." *Philosophy* 59 (1984): 431–42.

*Mohanty, J. N. "Rorty, Phenomenology and Transcendental Philosophy." *Journal of the British Society for Phenomenology* 14 (1983): 91–98.

*Murphy, Chris. Critical notice on *Mirror*. *Australasian Journal of Philosophy* 59 (1981): 338–45.

*Murray, Gilbert. "The Failure of Nerve." In *Five Stages of Greek Religion*. 3d ed. Doubleday/Anchor, 1951.

*_____. "Pagan Religion and Philosophy at the Time of Christ." In *Humanist Essays*. Allen and Unwin, 1964.

*Nielsen, Kai. "Scientism, Pragmatism and the Fate of Philosophy." Forthcoming in *Inquiry*.

_____. "How to be Skeptical About Philosophy." Forthcoming in *Philosophy*.

*_____. "Can There Be Progress in Philosophy?" Forthcoming in *Metaphilosophy*.

_____. "Rorty and the Self-Image of Philosophy." Forthcoming in *International Journal of Philosophy*.

*Nietzsche, Friedrich. *Daybreak*. Translated by R. J. Hollingdale. Cambridge University Press, 1982.

*Plato. *Sophist*. In Francis Cornford, *Plato's Theory of Knowledge*. Bobbs-Merrill, 1957.

*Portmess, Lisa. "An Historicist View of Teaching Philosophy." *Teaching Philosophy* 7 (1984): 313–23.

Prado, C. G. Review of "Philosophy and the Mirror of Nature." *Queen's Quarterly* 88 (1981): 591–93.

*_____. "Rorty's Pragmatism." *Dialogue* 22 (1983): 441–50.

*_____. *Making Believe: Philosophical Reflections on Fiction*. Greenwood Press, 1984.

*_____. "The Need for Truth." *Dialogue* 23 (1984): 687–88.

*_____. "Hermeneutics, Analysis and the Religious." Paper read at the 15th

Congress of the International Association for the History of Religions, Sydney, Australia, August 1985.

*_____. *Rethinking How We Age: A New View of the Aging Mind.* Greenwood Press, 1986.

*Putnam, Hilary. *Meaning and the Moral Sciences.* Cambridge University Press, 1978.

*Quine, Willard van Orman. "Two Dogmas of Empiricism." Reprinted in *From a Logical Point of View.* 2d ed. Harvard University Press, 1961.

Rorty, Richard. "Experience and the Analytic: A Reconsideration of Empiricism" (review). *International Journal of Ethics* 70 (1959): 75–7.

_____. "John Dewey: His Thought and Influence" (review). *Teacher's College Record* 62 (1960): 88–9.

_____. "Modern Science and Human Freedom" (review). *International Journal of Ethics* 70 (1960): 248–49.

_____. "Pragmatism, Categories and Language." *Philosophical Review* 70 (1961): 197–223.

_____. "Recent Metaphilosophy." *Review of Metaphysics* 15 (1961): 299–318.

_____. "The Limits of Reductionism." In *Experience, Existence and the Good,* edited by I. C. Lieb, 110–116. Southern Illinois Press, 1961.

_____. "Introduction to the Philosophy of History" (review). *The New Leader,* 25 December 1961, 18–19.

_____. "American Pragmatism: Peirce, James and Dewey" (review). *International Journal of Ethics* 72 (1962): 146–47.

_____. "The Value Judgment" (review). *Journal for the Scientific Study of Religion* 2 (1962): 139–140.

_____. "Realism, Categories, and the Linguistic Turn." *International Philosophical Quarterly* 2 (1962): 307–322.

_____. "Utopian Essays and Practical Proposals" (review). *Teacher's College Record* 64 (1963): 743–44.

_____. "The Subjectivist Principle and the Linguistic Turn." In *Alfred North Whitehead: Essays on His Philosophy,* edited by George Kline. Prentice-Hall, 1963.

_____. "Matter and Event." In *The Concept of Matter,* edited by Ernan McMullin, 407–524. Notre Dame University Press, 1963.

_____. "Empiricism, Extensionalism and Reductionism." *Mind* 72 (1963): 176–86.

_____. "Understanding Whitehead" (review). *Journal of Philosophy* 60 (1963): 246–51.

_____. "Reason and Analysis" (review). *Journal of Philosophy* 60 (1963): 551–57.

_____. "Comments on Prof. Hartshorne's Paper." *Journal of Philosophy* 60 (1963): 606–08.

_____. "Chauncy Wright and the Foundations of Pragmatism" (review). *Philosophical Review* 73 (1964): 287–89.

_____. Several paragraphs in *Philosophical Interrogations*, edited by Beatrice Rome and Sidney Rome. Holt, Rinehart and Winston, 1964.

_____. "Clarity Is not Enough: Essays in Criticism of Linguistic Philosophy" (review). *International Philosophical Quarterly* 4 (1964): 623–24.

_____. "Mind-Body Identity, Privacy and Categories." *Review of Metaphysics* 19 (1965): 25–54.

_____. Article on Aristotle in *The American Peoples' Encyclopedia*, edited by Walter D. Scott. Spencer Press, 1966.

_____. "Charles Peirce and Scholastic Realism" (review). *Philosophical Review* 75 (1966): 116–19.

_____. Articles on "Intuition" and "Relations, Internal and External" in *The Encyclopedia of Philosophy*, edited by Paul Edwards. Macmillan and Free Press, 1967.

_____. "Metaphysics, Reference and Language" (review). *Journal of Philosophy* 64 (1967): 770–74.

_____. "Do Analysts and Metaphysicians Disagree?" *Proceedings of the Catholic Philosophical Association* 41 (1967): 39–53.

_____. "Science and Metaphysics" (review). *Philosophy* 45 (1970): 66–70.

_____. "In Defense of Eliminative Materialism." *Review of Metaphysics* 24 (1970): 112–21.

_____. "Strawson's Objectivity Argument." *Review of Metaphysics* 24 (1970): 207–44.

_____. "Cartesian Epistemology and Changes in Ontology." In *Contemporary American Philosophy*, edited by John E. Smith, 273–92. Humanities Press, 1970.

_____. "Incorrigibility as the Mark of the Mental." *Journal of Philosophy* 67 (1970): 399–429.

_____. "Wittgenstein, Privileged Access, and Incommunicability." *American Philosophical Quarterly* 7 (1970): 192–205.

_____. "Verificationism and Transcendental Arguments." *Nous* 5 (1971): 3–14.

_____. "Ayer's *Origins of Pragmatism*" (review). *Philosophical Review* 80 (1971): 96–100.

————. "Functionalism, Machines, and Incorrigibility." *Journal of Philosophy* 69 (1972): 203–220.

————. "Dennett on Awareness." *Philosophical Studies* 23 (1972): 153–62.

————. "The World Well Lost." *Journal of Philosophy* 69 (1972): 649–65.

Rorty, Richard, and M. Natanson. "Nihilism" (review). *The Philosophy Forum* 11 (1972): S96–S108.

Rorty, Richard. "Indeterminacy of Translation and of Truth." *Synthese* 23 (1972): 443–62.

————. "Criteria and Necessity." *Nous* 7 (1973): 313–29.

————. "Genus as Matter: A Reading of Metaphysics Z-H." In *Exegesis and Argument: Studies in Greek Philosophy Presented to Gregory Vlastos*, edited by Richard Rorty, E. N. Lee, and A. P. D. Mourelatos, 393–420. Van Gorcum, 1973.

————. "More on Incorrigibility." *Canadian Journal of Philosophy* 4 (1974): 195–97.

————. "Matter as Goo." *Synthese* 25 (1974): 71–77.

————. "Keeping Philosophy Pure." *The Yale Review* 65 (1976): 336–56.

————. "Reference and Realism." *The Monist* 59 (1976): 321–40.

————. "Realism and Necessity: Milton Fisk's *Nature and Necessity*" (review). *Nous* 10 (1976): 345–54.

————. "Professionalized Philosophy and Transcendentalist Culture." *The Georgia Review* 30 (1976): 757–69.

————. "Overcoming the Tradition: Heidegger and Dewey." *Review of Metaphysics* 30 (1976): 280–305.

————. "Wittgensteinian Philosophy and Empirical Psychology." *Philosophical Studies* 31 (1977): 151–72.

————. "Dewey's Metaphysics." In *New Studies in the Philosophy of John Dewey*, edited by Steven Cahn, 45–74. Universities of New England Press, 1977.

————. "Ian Hacking's *Why Does Language Matter to Philosophy?*" (review). *Journal of Philosophy* 74 (1977): 416–32.

————. "Derrida on Languages, Being and Abnormal Philosophy." *Journal of Philosophy* 74 (1977): 673–81.

————. "Epistemological Behaviorism and the De-Transcendentalization of Analytic Philosophy." *Neue Hefte für Philosophie* 14 (1978): 117–42.

————. "A Middle Ground Between Neurons and Holograms?" *The Behavioral and Brain Sciences* 2 (1978): 248.

————. "Philosophy as a Kind of Writing: An Essay on Derrida." *New Literary History* 10 (1978): 141–60. (Reprinted in *Consequences*)

_____. "Transcendental Arguments, Self-reference, and Pragmatism." In *Transcendental Arguments and Science*, edited by Peter Bieri, Rolf Horstman, and Lorenz Kreuger, 77–103. Dordrecht, 1979.

_____. "The Unnaturalness of Epistemology." In *Body, Mind and Method: Essays in Honor of Virgil C. Aldrich*, edited by Donald Gustafson and Bangs Tapscott, 77–92. Dordrecht, 1979.

_____. "From Epistemology to Hermeneutics." *Acta Philosophica Fennica* 30 (1979): 11–30.

*_____. *Philosophy and the Mirror of Nature*. Princeton University Press, 1979.

_____. "De l'epistemologie à l'hermeneutique." *Dialectica* 33 (1979): 165–88. (Translation of "From Epistemology to Hermeneutics")

_____. "Pragmatism, Relativism and Irrationalism." *Proceedings and Addresses of the American Philosophical Association* 53 (1980): 719–38.

_____. "Idealism, Holism, and the 'Paradox of Knowledge.'" In *The Philosophy of Brand Blanshard*, edited by P. A. Schlip, 719–38. La Salle, 1980.

_____. "Kripke vs. Kant" (review). *London Review of Books*, 4 September 1980.

_____. "On Worldmaking" (review). *The Yale Review* 66 (1980): 276–79.

*_____. "Reply to Taylor and Dreyfus." In symposium "What is Hermeneutics?" *Review of Metaphysics* 34 (1980): 39–56.

_____. "Searle and the Secret Powers of the Brain." *The Behavioral and Brain Sciences* 3 (1980): 445–46.

_____. *Der Spiegel der Natur: Eine Kritik der Philosophie*. Suhrkamp, 1981. (Translation of *Mirror*)

*_____. "Is There a Problem about Fictional Discourse?" *Funktionen des Fictiven: Poetik und Hermeneutik* 10 (1981). Fink Verlag. (Reprinted in *Consequences*)

_____. "Freud, Morality, and Hermeneutics." *New Literary History* 12 (1981): 177–85.

_____. "Phenomenology and Pragmatism: A Reply to Yolton." *Philosophical Books* 22 (1981): 134–35.

_____. "Nineteenth-Century Idealism and Twentieth-Century Textualism." *The Monist* 64 (1981): 155–74.

_____. "From Epistemology to Romance: Cavell on Scepticism." *Review of Metaphysics* 34 (1981): 759–74. (Titled "Cavell on Skepticism" in *Consequences*)

_____. "Beyond Marx and Nietzsche" (review). *London Review of Books*, 19 February 1981, 5–6.

*_____. "Method, Social Science, and Social Hope." *The Canadian Journal of Philosophy* 11 (1981): 569–88. (Reprinted in *Consequences*)

———. "Being Business" (review). *Times Literary Supplement*, 3 July 1981, 760.

———. "Die Gegenwartslage der amerikanischen Philosophie." *Analyse & Kritik* 3 (1981): 3–22. (Translation of "Philosophy in America Today")

———. "Criticism Without Theory." Read at the *Modern Language Association* Convention, New York, New York, 28 December 1981.

*———. "Philosophy in America Today." *The American Scholar* (1982: 183–200). (Reprinted in *Consequences*)

*———. *Consequences of Pragmatism: Essays 1972–80*. University of Minnesota Press, 1982.

———. "Persuasive Philosophy" (review). *London Review of Books*, May/June 1982, 10–11.

———. "The Fate of Philosophy." *The New Republic*, 18 October 1982, 28–34.

———. "Contemporary Philosophy of Mind." *Synthese* 33 (1982): 323–48.

———. "Mind as Ineffable." In *Mind in Nature*, edited by Richard Elvee, 60–95. Nobel Conference 17, 1982. (Same as "Contemporary Philosophy of Mind")

———. "Brute and Raw Experience" (review). *The New Republic*, 6 December 1982, 33–36.

*———. "Relativism." The Howison Lecture, University of California at Berkeley, 31 January 1983.

———. "Unsoundness in Perspective" (review). *The Times Literary Supplement*, 17 June 1983, 619–20.

———. "Against Belatedness" (review). *The London Review of Books*, June/July 1983, 3–5.

———. "What Are Philosophers For?" *The Center Magazine*, September/October 1983, 40–44.

———. "Solidarite ou Objectivite?" *Critique*, December 1983, 923–40.

———. "Pragmatism Without Method." In *Sidney Hook: Philosopher of Democracy and Humanism*, edited by Paul Kurtz, 259–73. Prometheus, 1983.

*———. "Postmodernist Bourgeois Liberalism." *The Journal of Philosophy* 80 (1983): 583–89.

*———. "A Reply To Six Critics." *Analyse & Kritik* 6 (1984): 78–98.

———. "Habermas, Lyotard et la postmodernite" (review). *Critique*, March 1984, 181–97.

———. "Habermas and Lyotard on Post-Modernity." *Praxis International*, April 1984, 32–44.

———. "Life at the End of Inquiry" (review). *London Review of Books*, August/ September 1984, 6–7.

———. "Deconstruction and Circumvention." *Critical Inquiry*, September 1984, 1–23.

———. "Solidarity or Objectivity." *Nanzan Review of American Studies* 6 (1984): 1–19.

———. "Signposts Along the Way That Reason Went" (review). *London Review of Books*, February 1984, 5–6.

———. "What's It All About?" (review). *London Review of Books*, May/June 1984, 3–4.

———. "Heidegger Wider den Pragmatisten." *Neue Hefte für Philosophie* 22 (1984): 1–22.

———. "The Historiography of Philosophy: Four Genres." In *Philosophy in History*, edited by Richard Rorty, J. B. Schneewind, and Q. Skinner, 49–75. Cambridge University Press, 1984.

*———. "Comments on Sleeper and Edel." *Transactions of the Charles S. Peirce Society* 21 (1985): 40–48.

———. "Traditional and Analytical Philosophy: Lectures on the Philosophy of Language" (review). *Journal of Philosophy* 82 (1985): 720–29.

*———. "Science as Solidarity." Read at McMaster University, Hamilton, Ontario, 20 January 1986.

*———. "Freud and Moral Reflection." John Milton Scott Lecture, Queen's University, Kingston, Ontario, 23 January 1986.

*———. "Texts and Lumps." Forthcoming in *New Literary History*.

*———. "Pragmatism, Davidson and Truth." Forthcoming in a *Festschrift* for Davidson, edited by Ernest LePore. University of Minnesota Press.

———. "Heidegger Against the Pragmatists." To be incorporated into the book on Heidegger, circulating as a mimeographed copy first made available in a seminar on Heidegger, Winter 1981, Princeton University.

———. "Heidegger Glossary." An amusing compendium of "definitions" of Heideggerian terms, this is circulating in mimeograph form.

———. ed. *The Linguistic Turn: Recent Essays in Philosophical Method.* University of Chicago Press, 1967.

Rotenstreich, Nathan. "Rorty's Interpretation of Hegel." *Review of Metaphysics* 39 (1985): 321–33.

*Schwartz, Robert. Review of *Mirror*. *The Journal of Philosophy* 80 (1983): 51–67.

*Skinner, Quentin. "The End of Philosophy?" *New York Review*, 19 March 1981.

*Taylor, Charles. "Understanding in Human Sciences." *Review of Metaphysics* 34 (1980): 25–38.

*_____. "Minerva Through the Looking Glass." *Times Literary Supplement*, 26 December 1980.

*Wiener, Phillip. "Pragmatism." In *Dictionary of the History of Ideas*. Charles Scribner's Sons, 1973.

*Williams, Bernard. "Auto-da-Fe." *New York Review* 28 April 1983.

*Young, James. "Pragmatism and the Fate of Philosophy." *Dialogue* 23 (1984): 683–86.

Index

Interpretation
  correction interpretation, Rorty's,
    46
  hermeneutics, Gadamer's, 32–34
  pragmatism, 44, 135
  reading is interpreting, Gadamer
    and Rorty belief, 46
  test for, 47
  Rorty's, of Dewey, criticized,
    120–121
  truth by Meynell, 13
Intralinguistic. *See* Language
Intuition, 37–38, 57

J

James, William
  conversation, changes in, 157
  guarantees not offered, 157
  pragmatic arguments for religious
    faith, 80
  pragmatism of, 63, 157
  Rorty on, 41, 157, 158
  truth, view on, 32
Jones, Peter, 47, 122

K

Kant, Immanuel
  differentiation between concepts
    and intuitions, 57
  Kantian distinction, abandonment
    of, 75
  notion of "conceptual frameworks"
    and language, 59
  skepticism and Cavell, 69
  sense of truth, 25
Knowledge
  authority in, Prado, 136
  growth of, 123–124, 137–138, 150
  history of, Nietzsche's contention,
    26
  metanarratives and, Rorty, 136
  mirroring nature, 25
  Prado on, 136
  Rorty notion of, Edel's charge, 121
  what counts as, 125
  weakening of, 123

Kuhn, Thomas, 98, 101
  Kuhnian paradigm shifts, 71, 127,
    148

L

Laissez faire, optimism or economic
  individualism, 99–100
Language
  as medium of understanding,
    Gadamer, 74
  as replication, and philosophical
    contentions about intelligibility,
    118
  basic ostensions, 58
  "conceptual framework" and, 59
  correspondence of, 20, 30, 38
  Davidson and, 56–61, 146
    holistic view of language, 56–61
  intralinguistic nature of truth,
    31–32, 46, 55
  "language is the house of Being,"
    Heidegger, 74
  linguistics
    extralinguistics component, world
      determining true belief, 88
    field linguistics and Davidson's
      view of truth, 63
    linguistic practice and
      intralinguistic criteria in place
      of correspondence, 27, 31
    philosophical theory and, 75
    truth in terms of, 38
  meanings, 59
  medium of being, Gadamer's
    conception of language, 34
  metaphors, 132
    root-metaphors, discourse
      generated by, 147
  metaphor-sets, 132, 145, 147–149
  methodology for production of, 125
  neutral
    impossibility, effect on
      objectivity, 123
    vocabulary, 136
  pairing off, 38, 40
  philosophical theory and linguistics,
    75